T0245796

HBR Guide to
Executing
Your Strategy

Harvard Business Review Guides

Arm yourself with the advice you need to succeed on the job, from the most trusted brand in business. Packed with how-to essentials from leading experts, the HBR Guides provide smart answers to your most pressing work challenges.

The titles include:

HBR Guide for Women at Work

HBR Guide to Being a Great Boss

HBR Guide to Being More Productive

HBR Guide to Better Business Writing

HBR Guide to Better Mental Health at Work

HBR Guide to Building Your Business Case

HBR Guide to Buying a Small Business

HBR Guide to Changing Your Career

HBR Guide to Coaching Employees

HBR Guide to Collaborative Teams

HBR Guide to Data Analytics Basics for Managers

HBR Guide to Dealing with Conflict

HBR Guide to Delivering Effective Feedback

HBR Guide to Emotional Intelligence

HBR Guide to Executing Your Strategy

HBR Guide to Finance Basics for Managers

HBR Guide to Getting the Mentoring You Need

HBR Guide to Getting the Right Job

HBR Guide to Getting the Right Work Done

HBR Guide to
Executing Your Strategy

HARVARD BUSINESS REVIEW PRESS

Boston, Massachusetts

Copyright 2023 Harvard Business School Publishing Corporation

All rights reserved

Printed in the United States of America

10 9 8 7 6 5 4 3 2 1

The web addresses referenced in this book were live and correct at the time of the book's publication but may be subject to change.

Library of Congress Cataloging-in-Publication Data

Names: Harvard Business Review Press, issuing body.
Title: HBR guide to executing your strategy.
Other titles: Harvard Business Review guide to executing your
    strategy | Harvard business review guides.
Description: Boston, Massachusetts : Harvard Business Review Press,
    [2023] | Series: HBR guides | Includes index. |
Identifiers: LCCN 2023006837 (print) | LCCN 2023006838 (ebook) |
    ISBN 9781647825157 (paperback) | ISBN 9781647825164 (epub)
Subjects: LCSH: Strategic planning. | Business planning. | Industrial
    management. | Executive ability. | Success in business.
Classification: LCC HD30.28 .H39345 2023 (print) | LCC HD30.28
    (ebook) | DDC 658.4/012--dc23/eng/20230417
LC record available at https://lccn.loc.gov/2023006837
LC ebook record available at https://lccn.loc.gov/2023006838

ISBN: 978-1-64782-515-7
eISBN: 978-1-64782-516-4

The paper used in this publication meets the requirements of the American National Standard for Permanence of Paper for Publications and Documents in Libraries and Archives Z39.48-1992.

What You'll Learn

It's been said that execution is where strategy goes to die. That may sound dramatic, but even the best strategies can falter when it's time to translate them into action. Objectives are misunderstood, initiatives lose their focus, and volatile environments strain organizations past their ability to adapt.

Just as strategy is unique to every company, so is execution. But there are essential parts of the process you need to know to ensure your plan moves forward. To start, you must fully understand the details of your strategy and use that information to align your organization and identify the capabilities you have—and need. You must communicate strategic objectives clearly, setting your employees' direction and helping them manage multiple strategic projects all at once. And you must track performance and manage across silos to ensure the entire organization is working toward common goals.

This book provides the advice you need to ensure that you successfully execute your strategy. You'll learn how to:

- Fully understand your strategy and how its pieces fit together

- Assess strategic alignment across your company

- Evaluate organizational capabilities and identify areas for improvement

- Communicate the "why" behind your strategy and rally people behind it

- Translate strategy into specific action items for your team

- Prioritize your projects at both the strategic and operational levels

- Allow room for experimentation to enhance creativity and adaptability

- Define metrics for performance that ensure the results you want

- Eliminate cross-departmental rivalries and reduce the perception of conflicting goals

- Identify when—and how—to change your strategy

Contents

Contents

Contents

SECTION SEVEN

When Your Strategy Needs to Change

Getting Started

CHAPTER 1

Closing the Chasm Between Strategy and Execution

by Doug Sundheim

Setting strategy is elegant. It's a clean and sophisticated process of collecting and analyzing data, generating insights, and identifying smart paths forward. Done at arm's length in an academic fashion, tight logic is the only glue needed to hold ideas together. The output is a smooth narrative in a professional-looking document made up of Venn diagrams, 2×2 matrixes, and high-level plans of attack. *Jettison this business. Focus efforts here. Build up this organizational capability.* Executives buy

Adapted from content posted on hbr.org, August 22, 2013 (product #H00B51).

into the plan. The strategists, confident in their intellectual prowess, quietly recede into the background.

Then the trouble starts. Execution is a minefield. The clean and elegant logic of strategy gets dirty in the real world. Agendas compete. Priorities clash. Decisions stall. Communication breaks down. Time lines get blown. It's never a question of *if* these problems will happen; it's a question of when and to what degree. Managing these challenges takes street smarts and muscle. Overwhelming success means you take a few punches, but still make the plan happen. The process is always a little ugly. The executors' dirt-in-the-fingernails view on the ground is much different from the strategists' high-minded view from the air.

The implication is obvious—strategists and executors must work together better to bridge these two worlds. It's common sense. Unfortunately, it's far from common practice. What typically happens is an awkward handoff between the two. In the worst cases the strategists adopt an elitist, disconnected mindset: *We're the idea people, someone else will make it happen.* They don't bother to truly understand what it takes to implement the ideas. They don't engage the executors early and ask, "How will this actually work?" The executors contribute to the trouble as well. Often they don't truly understand the thinking behind the strategy. They take it at face value and don't ask enough tough questions.

When things fall apart, each points a finger at the other side.

The easy solutions for this divide are the process solutions: better project management, clearer rules of engagement, and tighter operating policies. The tougher (and more powerful) solutions are the cultural ones: getting each side to actually care about what the other side is doing. Not just from a lip-service perspective, but from a fundamental belief that my success is inextricably tied to yours so I better engage with you.

Strategy and execution are a false dichotomy, unnaturally sheared apart to divide labor in increasingly complex organizations. It's an efficient approach. Alone, the shearing isn't a problem. The problem is that both sides don't see it as their responsibility to intelligently pull the two sides back together again. They leave a chasm, hoping that it will miraculously close on its own. It never does. Things just fall through it.

The best strategists and executors don't see a handoff between strategy and execution. They see an integrated whole. They continuously hand ideas back and forth throughout all phases of a project, strengthening them together. They fight to bring each other closer. Over the years, I've noticed that the best strategists and executors believe certain things that drive their success—things that mediocre strategists and executors don't believe.

The best strategists believe:

- **If I can't see and articulate how we're actually going to make this strategy work, it probably won't.** Smart strategists know that there are a lot of gaps, holes, and challenges in their strategies. They tirelessly keep a critical eye on the viability of their plans and stay curious—continuously asking themselves and others, how will this really work?

When they find issues, they team up with the executors and get out in front of them.

- **While it's painful to integrate execution planning into my strategizing, it's even more painful to watch my strategies fail.** Most strategists dislike execution planning. It's a tedious process for someone who likes to think about big ideas. But good strategists understand that they have unique insights into the strategy that executors will miss, usually to disastrous ends. So they stay engaged.

- **Sounding smart is overrated. Doing smart is where the real value lies.** Effective strategists aren't full of themselves. They realize their ideas are just that—ideas. They know that if they're not executed well, their strategies are nothing more than daydreams.

- **I'm just as responsible for strong execution as the executor is.** This is a powerful mindset to hold. The best strategists see themselves as leaders, not merely thinkers. They feel their job is to deliver results, not just ideas.

The best executors believe:

- **I need to be involved in the strategy process early— even if that means I have to artfully push my way into it.** It'd be easy if executors naturally had a seat at the strategy table. Unfortunately, they often don't. Many still receive strategies as a handoff.

Smart executors don't tolerate this. They figure out how to get into the strategy process early.

- **I need to be perceived as relevant and valuable to the strategy process.** Smart executors know that they must earn a seat at the strategy table by actually adding value. They must move things forward by providing relevant and thoughtful considerations that strengthen the strategy. They can't show up and "just listen" in strategy meetings or else they won't be invited back.

- **I need to know the "whys" behind the strategy.** Smart executors want to know the intent behind the strategy. They want to know the thinking that drove certain choices. They know that this knowledge is crucial to making tough judgment calls when circumstances change down the implementation road (as they inevitably do).

- **I'm just as responsible for strong strategy as the strategist is.** The best executors see themselves as leaders, not merely implementers. They feel their job is to deliver strategic advantage for the organization, not just a project.

You can see a clear thread of responsibility running throughout all the beliefs above. Not responsibility for a given task, but rather responsibility for the *not-given* tasks—the messy spots in the middle where it's not clear who should own something. The best strategists, executors, and leaders stand up and say, "I'm responsible for it" even if it isn't in their job description. It's doubly powerful when both strategists and executors do this, meeting in the middle. That's true collaborative leadership.

Doug Sundheim is a leadership and strategy consultant. His latest book is *Taking Smart Risks: How Sharp Leaders Win When Stakes Are High*. Find out more about his services at www.sundheimgroup.com.

CHAPTER 2

What Is Execution, Exactly?

by Ken Favaro

It is striking how much confusion there is between strategy and execution. Is "strategy" a matter of making choices about where we want to go or want to become, where we play, and how we win, of setting goals and actions, about how we create and capture economic value over time? Does it include creating solutions to unforeseen problems and running with unexpected opportunities? Is "getting things done" what we mean by execution? Do you "execute" or "implement" a strategy? And can you separate these from strategy formation? Where

Adapted from "Defining Strategy, Implementation, and Execution," on hbr.org, March 31, 2015 (product #H01YRY).

does strategy end, execution begin, and implementation fit in?

For strategy wonks like me, thinking about the definitions of these ideas provides endless fascination. For many business leaders, however, the semantics matter a lot less. And that's too bad, because the semantics should matter. There are meaningful distinctions between the terms *strategy*, *implementation*, and *execution* that are helpful to running an enterprise in the real world. Ignoring, blurring, or getting them wrong creates sloppy thinking, deciding, and doing at all levels of an organization.

Let's start with *strategy*. As I understand the term, it consists of two categories: corporate strategy and business unit strategy. *Corporate strategy* consists of CEOs and top executives making just three basic choices:

- What should be the capabilities that distinguish the company?

- What should be the company's comparative advantage in adding value to its individual businesses?

- What businesses should the company be in?

These are the fundamental choices that a *corporate strategy* comprises, and they should frame and guide all the decisions that a company's corporate executives, functions, and staff make every day, including how they run the place, what they buy and sell, what markets they enter, how they measure success, and so on.

For a business unit within a company, there are also three key choices that cannot be delegated by its leaders. They are different but no less fundamental:

- Who should be the customers that define our target market?

- What should be the value proposition that differentiates our products and services with those customers?

- What should be the capabilities that make our business better than any other in marketing, selling, and delivering that value proposition?

These are the choices that a *business unit strategy* comprises, and they should drive the decisions a business unit's management team, functions, and staff make every day, including pricing, R&D, where to manufacture, and many more.

This brings me to *implementation. Merriam-Webster* defines it as "putting something into effect." For our purposes, this means taking the decisions and actions that are necessary to turn the two kinds of strategy choices I've just described into reality. If the corporation has the capabilities, enterprise advantage, and business portfolio it wants, its strategy is implemented. If the business unit has the customers, value proposition, and skills it has chosen to have, its strategy is also fully implemented.

Of course, almost by definition, a strategy can never actually be fully implemented because everything that you necessarily assumed when formulating it—about customers, technology, regulation, competitors, and so on—is in a constant state of flux. CEOs and their business unit leaders must continuously evolve their strategies (that is, those fundamental choices I mentioned before) if they are to remain relevant and competitive. And if that's the case, there will always be a gap between where their companies are and what their strategies call for. Closing that gap is "implementation." Thus, strategy and implementation are running almost continuously in parallel rather than in sequence.

What, then, is *execution*? Turning again to *Merriam-Webster*, "execution" is listed as a synonym for implementation, which may explain why these two words are so often used interchangeably. But *Merriam-Webster* actually defines execution as "performance"—to execute is to perform. So I define the term as the decisions and activities you undertake in order to turn your strategy and its implementation into commercial success. To achieve "execution excellence" is to realize the best possible results a strategy and its implementation will allow.

To understand what all this means, let's say that Netflix has made a corporate strategy choice to enter the content business and to exit the mail-order business. Once Netflix is in the content business and out of the mail-order business, that "strategy" (or that part of its strategy) is implemented. Now, it must do things such as set goals and plans for the content business, establish the right incentives, create a motivational, purpose-redolent mission statement, and other such things that leaders do to get the most out of their companies. Those are all activities needed to produce results within the context of an ever-evolving strategy and its ongoing implementation. This is execution.

Strategy, implementation, and execution are three coincident determinants of a company or business unit's ultimate output—its results—that are very difficult to parse into their individual effects. When we see a company or business unit producing poor results over multiple years, no one can say for sure whether that's due to poor strategy, implementation, or execution. But in my experience, it's very difficult to implement a poor strategy well and doubly difficult to produce excellent results with a poor strategy that's being poorly implemented. (Of course, having a great strategy is no guarantee of great results either; you still have to implement and execute well.)

The distinctions I make here are not between thinking and doing, or deciding and acting, or planning and producing. All of these kinds of activities are involved in strategy, implementation, and execution. Does that make them the same thing? Absolutely not. They each involve very different specific activities, tools, and people. And when business leaders conflate strategy, implementation, and execution, they usually end up with a lot of the trappings of running a modern-day enterprise—such as goals and targets; plans and initiatives; and mission, vision, and purpose statements—but very little actual strategy, implementation, or successful execution.

Lim Chow Kiat, longtime group investment officer and CEO at Singapore's GIC, says that for his organization "nomenclature is destiny. . . . We are meticulous about word choice. . . . The wrong words can corrode, if not corrupt, our [business.]" Charles Handy, the celebrated business guru, expressed a similar view in his *21 Letters on Life and Its Challenges*: "Words do matter. They change behavior. They shape our thinking because of the implicit messages they send; then our thoughts shape our actions. Always watch your language lest you send messages never intended."

Leaders should heed Kiat and Handy by being thoughtful and explicit about what they mean by strategy, implementation, and execution. Their people, directors, and owners will be grateful for the clarity and results it yields.

Ken Favaro is the lead principal of act2, an independent adviser based in Bronxville, New York; a guest instructor at Stanford University's Graduate School of Business; and the author of the forthcoming book *On Strategy*.

CHAPTER 3

Why Strategy Execution Unravels—and What to Do About It

by Donald Sull, Rebecca Homkes, and Charles Sull

When global CEOs are surveyed about their biggest concerns, strategy execution tops the list, ahead of innovation, geopolitical instability, and top-line growth. It's no wonder we wrestle with execution. Several common beliefs about it are just plain wrong.

Adapted from "Why Strategy Execution Unravels—and What to Do About It" (video), on hbr.org, October 3, 2016.

Let's look at five of the most damaging myths that lead organizations to waste time and resources on the wrong issues, while ignoring the things that really matter.

Myth 1: Execution Equals Alignment

When execution falters, managers tend to assume there's a problem with alignment—the processes linking strategy to action up and down the hierarchy. But in most companies, alignment isn't broken, and misguided efforts to fix it make matters worse. As managers track more and more metrics and demand progress meeting after progress meeting, employees start to feel micromanaged. That stifles creativity and collaboration, putting even more of a drag on execution. Managers then press harder on alignment. It's a classic downward spiral.

Solution: Improve coordination across units

If alignment isn't the problem, what is? It's a failure to coordinate across the business. Only half of managers say they can count on colleagues in other functions and units to keep their commitments. Managers compensate with a host of dysfunctional behaviors, such as letting promises to customers slip. To get better at execution, we need better systems for managing across the organization.

Myth 2: Execution Means Sticking to the Plan

The second myth is that good execution requires staying true to an established plan and never deviating. Organizations spend huge amounts of time and energy mapping out who should do what and with what resources, but they can't anticipate every event. In volatile markets, managers and employees need to be agile, and that's not easy. Sometimes people move too slowly to seize opportunities or head off threats. Other times, they react quickly but lose sight of company strategy.

Solution: Reallocate resources—continually

The key to solving this problem is to keep reallocating resources. Dividing up funds, people, and managerial attention isn't a onetime decision. If we make adjustments as needs change, we'll be quicker to kill failing initiatives, and we'll do better at shifting people across units to support strategic priorities.

A word of warning, though: Being agile doesn't mean chasing every opportunity. Strategic focus is essential. Without it, resources go to the wrong projects, and key initiatives don't get what they need to win big.

Myth 3: Communication Equals Understanding

Here's a sobering statistic: Just half of C-suite executives say they have a good sense of how their companies' strategic priorities fit together. Matters are even worse further down the chain. When communications reach team leaders and frontline supervisors, only 16% feel they have a good grasp of how priorities fit together.

Part of the problem is that leaders focus on the *quantity* of messages—the number of emails, meetings, and so on. Then they add to the confusion by changing their messages and diluting them with peripheral concerns.

Consider what happened at one tech company's annual off-site. Senior leaders went to great pains to communicate the company's strategy to the managers in attendance, but they also introduced 11 corporate priorities, a list of core competencies, a set of corporate values, and 21 new strategic terms. Not surprisingly, the managers were baffled about what mattered.

Solution: Keep messages simple and consistent

Instead of worrying about the amount of communication, leaders should focus on helping people grasp what they're saying. They need to lead discussions throughout the organization about what the strategy is and what it means for managers and their teams. They'll head off a lot of misunderstanding if they stick with the core messages and keep them simple and consistent. Often less is more.

Myth 4: A Performance Culture Drives Execution

When execution fails, many leaders think a weak performance culture is to blame. But most companies are good at rewarding employees who hit their numbers. If anything, they focus *too* much on performance, which causes people to play it safe. Employees make conservative commitments, favor surefire cost-cutting over risky growth, and milk existing businesses, rather than try new models. All these behaviors undermine execution.

Solution: Reward behaviors that support execution

Organizations need to look beyond "hitting the numbers." They need to reward behaviors that support execution, such as ambition, agility, experimentation, and collaboration. If performance comes at the expense of these skills, it's counterproductive.

Myth 5: Execution Should Be Driven from the Top

The final myth about execution is that it should be driven from the top. That's a problem because it doesn't encourage middle managers to develop their decision-making skills, show initiative, or own their results. In a top-down culture, they're more inclined to escalate conflicts than to resolve them, so they may lose the ability to work things out with colleagues in other units.

Take this example from Larry Bossidy. As the CEO of AlliedSignal, he personally monitored the performance of managers several levels below him. It was the stereotypical "heroic" leader driving execution himself. This approach can work—but only for a while. As long as Bossidy was at the helm, AlliedSignal's stock outperformed the market. But when he retired, the stock fell.

Consider the many decisions and actions that are crucial to execution. They often involve hard trade-offs. For example, synching up with colleagues in another unit might slow a team down, or screening customer requests against strategy might mean turning away business. The leaders closest to the situation are the ones best qualified to make these difficult choices.

Solution: Have frontline managers make the tough calls

Execution should be driven from the middle with guidance from the top. Senior leaders can help by modeling teamwork and adding systems to facilitate coordination.

If our beliefs about execution are flawed and lead to distracted patterns, what needs to change? The starting point is to redefine execution. Let's view it as "seizing strategic opportunities while coordinating across the company and adjusting as needed." Framing execution this way can help us avoid pitfalls, like rewarding performance alone and failing to adapt. And we'll get better at what really makes a difference: coordination, agility, and reallocating resources to our biggest strategic bets.

Donald Sull is a cofounder of CultureX and a senior lecturer at the MIT Sloan School of Management, where he directs the Culture 500 project. **Rebecca Homkes** is an executive strategy and growth adviser, a lecturer at the London Business School's Department of Strategy and Entrepreneurship, on the faculty at Duke Corporate Executive Education, and a previous fellow at the London School of Economics' Centre for Economic Performance. Her book on breakthrough growth during uncertainty is *Survive, Reset, Thrive*. **Charles Sull** is a cofounder of CultureX, where he advises C-suite leaders of leading companies about the best ways to build robust cultures that achieve strategic objectives. He helped develop the underlying AI platform at MIT that powers the CultureX platform and related research, which has reached an audience of millions and has been featured in the *New York Times*, *Wall Street Journal*, and Brené Brown's podcast.

Review the Specifics of Your Strategy

CHAPTER 4

Eight Questions to Ask About Your Company's Strategy

by Paul Leinwand and Matthias Bäumler

Companies often fail to address the tough questions about strategy and execution: Are we really clear, as a leadership team, about how we choose to create value in the marketplace? Can we articulate the few things the organization needs to do better than anyone else in order to deliver on that value proposition? Are we investing in those areas, and do they fit with most of the products and services we sell?

Adapted from "8 Tough Questions to Ask About Your Company's Strategy," on hbr.org, November 29, 2017 (product #H0414P).

TABLE 4-1

Tough questions to ask about your company's strategy

	Can we state it?	Do we live it?
Way to play	Are we clear about how we choose to create value in the marketplace?	Are we investing in the capabilities that really matter to our way to play?
Capabilities system	Can we articulate the three to six capabilities that describe what we do uniquely better than anyone else? Have we defined how they work together in a system? Do our strategy documents reflect this?	Do all our businesses draw on this superior capabilities system? Do our organizational structure and operating model support and leverage it? Does our performance management system reinforce it?
Product and service fit	Have we specified our product and service "sweet spot"? Do we understand how to leverage the capabilities system in new or unexpected arenas?	Do most of the products and services we sell fit with our capabilities system? Are new products and acquisitions evaluated on the basis of their fit with the way to play and the capabilities system?
Coherence	Can everyone in the organization articulate our differentiating capabilities? Is our company's leadership reinforcing these capabilities?	Do we have a right to win in our chosen market? Do all of our decisions add to our coherence, or do some of them push us toward incoherence?

Source: Adapted from "The Coherence Premium," by Paul Leinwand and Cesare Mainardi, *Harvard Business Review*, June 2010.

If your answer is yes to these and the other tough questions in table 4-1, you're among the select few. In our experience, few companies are asking or answering these fundamental questions critical to establishing a viable, thriving future for any organization.

Why is that? Why is it so difficult for leaders to talk about these topics?

Perhaps most commonly, executives struggle to address these topics as the answers will require fundamental transformation that they are not ready for, or because they do not see a path toward real differentiation as they work to squeeze revenue and profit growth to meet shorter-term targets. In some cases, the senior team and CEO do not make the time for these debates, opting to delay the conversation. Other leaders may feel that it's not the right time to be asking these questions, perhaps rationalizing that the CEO has been at the helm of the company for a year or more and a strategy (which likely isn't sufficient) is already in place. They might feel that the time for asking these questions has already passed, and they don't want to come across as launching criticism. Some executives may in fact value the lack of strategic clarity because it allows them to pursue their own priorities. As for CEOs themselves, they often *do* ask these questions when they start in their roles but feel constrained by the boundaries handed to them—either an incoherent portfolio or strong short-term pressure to meet targets that diverts their attention.

The result is that tough questions about the linkage between strategy and execution often go unaddressed.

So what can companies do to build a culture of accountability around the most important strategic questions? Leaders should consider these tactics.

Create purpose for your leadership team

Ultimately, leadership teams are the group that should be held accountable to ask and answer these questions with clear direction from the CEO, but often do not prioritize or feel incented to work as a team in this way. The CEO has the opportunity to empower and provide the ambition for the leadership team to take on the company's purpose. By understanding that the organization's ability to survive—and thrive—in the future is at stake, many leadership teams rise to the challenge and begin to work together to build a more meaningful and insightful discussion on strategy, and recognize the role they all must play to help shape the company's future.

Build in time for strategic discussion

Next, create a process for the executive team to think through and discuss these fundamental questions. Unfortunately, the traditional approach to strategic planning (for those companies still completing these exercises) often doesn't provide room for these conversations because it tends to be bottom-up, financial, and incremental in nature. Instead, what is needed is a time and place for executives to step away from the day-to-day urgencies and discuss and debate these questions openly. One CEO we spoke with talked about the need for the leadership team to "perform and transform," and many companies actually divide governance and management so that there is a dedicated group and process for looking after the future, as well as managing the current business.

Similarly, use the budget process to ensure alignment to these questions. Cost is a powerful tool to invest in the future, but most budgets simply increment their way forward, disconnected from meaningful strategic direction. They can similarly be used to drive clarity and resolve uncertainty.

Engage the organization in the tough questions

Involve a larger part of the organization in a discussion about how the company is doing on strategy and execution. As in the annual employee survey, organizations should take the pulse around the most important strategic topics. A broader set of the organization will likely provide an incredibly honest perspective on these key questions, and your organization will in turn better understand the potentially vast challenges and opportunities that the entire company faces moving forward. Besides telling you what people think the company's main challenges are, it also helps create a climate where such questions can be—and are—raised.

Drive accountability and direction with the board

The board is the only group that would have the long-term focus (what we call "longitudinal sustenance") to be able to manage these kinds of questions over time—and many board members are uniquely qualified to help the executive team answer and challenge some of the most difficult questions of strategy. Instead of the old practice of merely reviewing the company's strategy, many boards set up a structured process with management to talk about strategy and the linkages to execution. Management could take the lead in these discussions and work with the board in picking topics where directors will have salient input. Even periodic, direct interviews and conversations, in which board members are asked about their concerns, are a powerful way to engage the board more effectively.

As leaders, we have a responsibility to answer these fundamental questions—even if the answers aren't easy or immediately practical. We have to create the room for this conversation, and we owe our shareholders, customers, and employees clear answers about why we exist and what we do every day to fulfill that purpose. Building mechanisms to encourage debate is the best way to bring these fundamental questions out of the shadows and move them to center stage where they belong.

———————

Paul Leinwand is the global managing director for capabilities-driven strategy and growth at Strategy&, PwC's strategy consulting business. He is a principal with PwC US, an adjunct professor of strategy at Northwestern University's Kellogg School of Management, and a coauthor of several books, including *Beyond Digital: How Great Leaders Transform Their Organizations and Shape the Future* and *Strategy That Works: How Winning Companies Close the Strategy-to-Execution Gap* (Harvard Business Review Press, 2021 and 2016, respectively). **Matthias Bäumler**, formerly of PwC, is an adviser to executives in resource and process industries. He has published articles on the topic of strategy, including "8 Tough Questions to Ask About Your Company's Strategy" and "The Future of Chemicals."

CHAPTER 5

Does Your Strategy Have a Spine?

by Rita McGrath

For all the ink spilled on the concept of strategy, it continually proves to be a surprisingly slippery idea. In practice, leaders often struggle to define and communicate strategies to their team. In their *Harvard Business Review* article, "Can You Say What Your Strategy Is?" David J. Collis and Michael G. Rukstad don't mince words: "Most executives cannot articulate the objective, scope, and advantage of their business in a simple statement. If they can't, neither can anyone else."

Here, I'm going to describe a document that you can think of as a bridge between your strategy and the

---

Adapted from content posted on hbr.org, June 29, 2022 (product #H07434).

seemingly endless communications you need to make to get various stakeholders comfortable with backing it. I call it a "strategy spine" because it describes how the strategy translates into specific flows of resources. Much as your own spine serves to tie together many different parts of your body to create capability for movement, a strategy spine shows key stakeholders exactly how all the pieces fit.

Back from the Future

Before you can start building your strategy spine, you need to be clear on objectives, scope, and key advantages for, say, a five-to-six-year time frame. An exercise that I recommend is for those who are involved with creating the strategy to write a story from the future. Write it as though an admiring reporter for a leading publication in your sector was telling the story of your success.

What would that world look like? What experiences would customers be having that they would be willing to pay for? Which ecosystem partners will you be collaborating with? What kind of environment is it going to be for your employees? If you are in a mission-driven organization, what kind of impact will you have had and for whom? Make sure that you mention the key decisions and resource allocation choices you have made along the way to that future success.

Through this process, what you will find is that you are going to be, intentionally or not, making choices about what things led to that success and what things could have detracted from it. Then, coming back to today, you can start to fill out your strategy spine document.

Creating the Strategy Spine

The strategy spine document consists of six elements:

1. **Sources of revenue:** At the end of the day, if you don't know where your critical resources are going to come from, you have a long way to go to creating a durable strategy. A basic question here is who is going to provide funds to you? Through what vehicles? For what reasons? Using what business model? This will structure the whole rest of the document, so it is critically important to be clear about this.

2. **Key assumptions:** By definition, a strategy that moves your organization into the future is preparing for a world that doesn't yet exist. In this part of the spine, you'll lay out the most important assumptions you are making with respect to your sources of revenue. A big tendency you'll have to resist is to get defensive if you are challenged on your assumptions—don't fall into the trap of trying to be right when what you should be doing is learning.

3. **Key goals by your time horizon:** Next, spell out the metrics that your stakeholder can use to determine whether you are making progress toward your key objectives, at some future point in time—say, in five years. Again, you'll be driving these metrics from your sources of revenue. The metrics may need to change over time as you convert your assumptions into knowledge, but

it's helpful to have them laid out in written form. Otherwise, you may find yourself in a world of constantly changing goalposts.

4. **Revenue implications by your time horizon:** Having identified the sources of revenue, key assumptions, and goals, you now want to articulate what this all means in terms of the revenue the strategy will be creating when you reach your desired time horizon. This is a discipline very much related to discovery-driven planning in which you define success before you start working on a plan in uncertain conditions.

5. **Necessary supporting investments:** This next step asks you to articulate the investments that are specific to creating a complete offering for each revenue provider. If you need to invest in technology, buy a physical asset, bring on a particular number of employees, whatever, this is where it belongs. What you want your stakeholder to understand is the connection between future potential revenue and investments made today.

6. **Additional infrastructure needs:** Aside from investments to support each revenue source, sometimes you need to make basic commitments to keeping things up to date. This may be investing to retire legacy systems, bringing physical infrastructure into the modern age, updating old equipment, and so on. The distinction here is

between stuff you need to invest in to operate at all and the things that are specific to a particular part of your strategy.

To show what an actual spine looks like, I'm going to look at a well-known firm tackling a big new opportunity. I'll begin by describing the firm's strategy, and I'll then fill out what could have been that company's strategy spine. (I should note that I am not working with the company referred to nor do I have any insider information.)

Unilever's Positive Beauty Growth Platform

In September 2021, consumer packaged goods giant Unilever kicked off a new venture called the Positive Beauty Growth Platform. It's part of a larger strategy for the firm that is aimed at linking together the twin issues of inequality and environmental sustainability. Sustainable brands already represent high-growth opportunities for the firm, as it reported in 2019 that its purpose-led brands have outperformed the others in its portfolio in terms of growth.[1]

The platform seeks to fund startups and scale-ups to give it a cutting-edge look at the changing way in which people are buying, most notably through mechanisms involving social connections. Grand View Research finds that this way of buying is worth about $474.8 billion in size as of 2021 but is slated to grow rapidly to some $3.4 trillion by 2028.[2] So this is a classic investment in a set of options—investments with huge upside potential that you can access with a relatively contained downside.

One would want to know, when doing this for real, what the objectives are for the project to contribute to the personal care division. Although I'm not privy to this information, we can play around a bit with what we do know. The division's revenue in 2019 was some $24.5 billion, and as of this writing, it has been growing successfully.[3]

Clearly, one of the goals of this strategy is to meet customers where they are—which increasingly is not in conventional retail outlets for the kinds of products Unilever sells. Indeed, Seb Joseph reports in *Digiday* that 8% of Unilever's total sales in 2020 were coming from e-commerce channels, as opposed to 6% the year before.[4] If we figure that by the time the strategy is mature, e-commerce of some kind will represent 10% of the division's sales, that implies investments to capture some $2.5 billion of consumer spending by those engaged in social activities combined with commerce.

A Hypothetical Strategy Spine

Table 5-1, "A strategy spine for Unilever," shows what it might look like, all filled out. Without insider knowledge, it's hard to put specific numbers and goals in the boxes, but I'll offer some illustrative examples.

How should you use the document? You can think of this as a living document bringing the principles of agile working to strategy—you can create one, learn more, get feedback, and update it as new information comes in. What it allows you to see, in a simple format, is how all the different pieces of revenue and investment fit together—or don't. You can now use it to work backward to

TABLE 5-1

A strategy spine for Unilever

Here's how Unilever might fill out the six components of a strategy spine for its Positive Beauty Growth Platform.

SOURCES OF SOCIAL REVENUE

	Livestreaming and shopping	Shoppable media	Gaming and e-commerce	Group buying
Key assumptions	Consumers will increasingly be influenced to buy personal care products accompanied by advice or demonstrations. Trusted influencers, not retail outlets, are the new gate-keepers. We can offer influencers enough value that they work with us without going independent. Users are motivated to order during the livestream or else miss out on deals.	The purchase experience will increasingly be integrated with content consumption, collapsing the traditional funnel. Fast-moving consumer goods (FMCG) companies can reduce ad spending if they can sell directly without ads. Working with other platforms can reduce our dependence on Big Tech companies such as Facebook and Google.	People already purchase digital products as part of playing games; this will extend to physical products as well. Partnerships with technology and game producers will yield ever-better platforms through which to sell our products. Even post-pandemic, gaming will continue to be an important way in which people (especially young people) socialize and connect.	The Tupperware buying experience can go digital. Group shopping proves attractive to shoppers looking for both social connections and other benefits (such as a discount). The community-buying model created by entities such as Kickstarter and GoFundMe takes off in other areas of commerce. Customers enticed to group buying by deals will make future purchases.

(continued)

TABLE 5-1

Sources of social revenue

	Livestreaming and shopping	Shoppable media	Gaming and e-commerce	Group buying
Illustrative key goals, 2026	Be present at 35% of all livestream events featuring our products or competitors' products. Be among the top five players in share of mind when users are logging on.	Have offers available for at least 50% of all target customers' content-consumption time.	Have partnership agreements with the five largest-footprint game developers.	Capture 25% or more of group-buying dollars for beauty and self-care products.
Revenue implications by 2026	Not specified; being an outsider I wouldn't know, but you'd want to put an aiming point for revenues from this revenue source for about five years out. Based on the previous information, the four sources of revenue would have to total to about $2.5 billion in new revenue (or retained revenue) to be considered successful.			
Specific supporting investments required	Create a tech stack that supports livestream shopping + livestreaming: video, product info, chat, reaction space, on-demand options, coupons, and purchase completion. Invest to create loyalty levels.	Integrate payment and fulfillment solutions across multiple platforms. Make prices, product information, and stock information consistent across platforms.	Offer partnerships and investments with game designers to make working with us attractive. Invest in the software needed to integrate purchasing into the gaming environment.	For this idea to work in the West, an omnipresent social commerce app, such as those currently at work in China, would need to be developed. Otherwise squad shopping is unlikely to take off.
Infrastructure	Flexible e-commerce systems that support multiple platforms Secure systems that are not vulnerable to hacking or misuse Back-end customer identification, loyalty, and group identification processes			

establish the annual metrics and goalposts that become part of your operating plan. This way, you can modify the plan as you test your assumptions and learn more about what is viable or not. Good luck!

———————

Rita McGrath is a professor at Columbia Business School and a globally recognized expert on strategy in uncertain and volatile environments. She is the author of *The End of Competitive Advantage* and, most recently, *Seeing Around Corners*.

NOTES

1. Unilever, "Unilever's Purpose-Led Brands Outperform," press release, June 11, 2019, https://www.unilever.com/news/press-and-media/press-releases/2019/unilevers-purpose-led-brands-outperform/.

2. Grand View Research, "Social Commerce Market Size, Share & Trends Analysis Report by Business Model, by Product Type, by Platform/Sale Channel, by Region, and Segment Forecasts, 2023–2030," 2018–2021, https://www.grandviewresearch.com/industry-analysis/social-commerce-market.

3. Tugba Sabanoglu, "Unilever's Personal Care Division Revenue Worldwide 2017 to 2021," Statistica, November 30, 2020, https://www.statista.com/statistics/254605/unilevers-skin-care-and-hair-care-market-share-worldwide/.

4. Seb Joseph, "'Retailers Are Media Owners in Their Own Right: Why E-commerce Is Driving More of Unilever's Media Spend," Digiday, September 9, 2020, https://digiday.com/media/retailers-are-media-owners-in-their-own-right-why-e-commerce-is-driving-more-of-unilevers-media-spend/.

CHAPTER 6

What You Lose with Your New Strategy

by Natalia Weisz and Roberto Vassolo

There is one key factor that strategic decision-makers often neglect in formulating and implementing their strategies: the crucial role and impact of loss.

Moving ahead on big new strategic priorities inevitably generates losses: Some parts of the organization, some people, functions, values, and traditions will be downgraded or even abandoned in the name of progress. Corporations trying to implement strategic initiatives typically trumpet the benefits and ignore these losses,

---

Adapted from content posted on hbr.org, July 13, 2022 (product #H074OP).

treating implementation as a straightforward technical challenge. Doing so is a comfortable default. It gives strategic change the illusion of a win-win: No one gets hurt, and nothing gets left behind.

It's a risky, even dangerous illusion. At its best, strategic planning involves informed conversations about the organization's future, resulting in a plan reflecting new priorities or reordering of old ones. For any strategy to be successful, executives need to identify, understand, and allocate time, attention, energy, and money for the losses the organization will face in pursuit of its new priorities. In this way, strategic planning can be seen as what Ron Heifetz, Marty Linsky, and Alexander Grashow have called an "adaptive challenge," helping the organization come to terms with new realities and to appropriately grieve what is lost.[1]

This adaptive challenge can be contrasted with mere "technical" work, in which the factors are known, and people continue in the same basic system and circumstances. This means bringing into the strategy planning process all the tools and frameworks that help teams and organizations deal with the losses that are part and parcel of doing adaptive work, and actively engaging those people for whom solutions will need to be internalized in minds, commitments, and behaviors.

Dealing with Direct and Indirect Loss

New strategic priorities require organizational changes. We all embrace change when we think it is going to be good for us. What we resist is loss. The latent and often unarticulated fear of loss is usually behind organizational inertia and resistance. Therefore, in any strategic planning process, it is essential to understand the relationship between the new priorities the context demands and the losses different groups within the organization will face when addressing these priorities.

Some types of losses are clear to detect and eventually address. For example, direct losses relating to power, money, prestige, career prospects, and autonomy come up quickly in planning conversations. More hidden are the competency losses. The fear of having to deal with new organizational demands can trigger significant anxiety. The pain associated with this real or perceived loss of competence can equal or even exceed that of direct losses. We still recall a manager at a major bank saying: "I'm 50 years old and I don't know whether I can develop the necessary skills for the changes to come." No one wishes to feel incompetent. However, adaptive challenges demand both experimentation and learning new competencies. They require endurance through painful periods of uncertainty generated by lack of knowledge and relevant skills. Digital transformation in the banking industry creates losses that are a big hurdle for those who have been in the industry for many years.

Loss of loyalty is another serious consideration. No person is an island. We have loyalties to those who share our values, interests, or history. If you're someone who serves as a voice for coworkers or friends, that means they expect you to defend certain values and perspectives. Upsetting those expectations can carry a high cost, mainly in terms of identity and a sense of belonging. A fear of eroding trust inhibits open conversations about the real work to be done. It undermines progress in strategic priorities.

Such losses are not evenly distributed, and they affect groups differently, varying in type and magnitude. That explains the different levels of commitment and resistance to priorities. The good news is that, just as you can anticipate new priorities in the face of a changing context, you can also anticipate the losses that these priorities will generate.

Building an Adaptive Strategic Planning Process

Understanding the relationship between priorities and losses can help senior management teams to make strategic planning processes more effective in mobilizing learning and change. Here are three steps you can take to help facilitate this.

Strengthen the holding environment

A holding environment is a safe space where executives can talk openly about what they don't know and what they need to learn, and where the deeper values that will be brought into play during this process can be made explicit. Without a minimum holding environment, the chances at true learning decrease and it becomes more difficult to form an adequate strategy with a coherent set of priorities.

You may never achieve the perfect holding environment, but you can nurture it until it is good enough. Do this by, first, showing genuine conviction in addressing the real challenges and the demands they imply in a caring way. Next, create some spatial and time boundaries. Knowing that certain issues must be resolved within a certain time and space helps focus and contain. Finally, foster emotional connection. For example, people who may have been working on the management team for years know less about their peers' histories, hopes, and fears than you might think. This emotional disconnection makes it challenging to show vulnerability and, in turn, to progress in collective learning. One of our favorite ways to strengthen the holding environment is to establish an initial moment for sharing personal stories. Before getting into the corporate needs, we invite managers to learn more from one another by sharing some intimate aspects of their past and present.

Establish a formal moment to discuss losses

Remember that systems, including organizations, can develop the capacity to handle all kinds of challenges—but only those they can name. What we do not recognize and name will later emerge in numerous forms of resistance. So, leaders need to make this naming a formal step or goal. While priorities are discussed and agreed upon, the conversation must move from the purely analytic elements of strategy to putting real names and faces to those who would have to implement, manage, and bear the consequences of the decisions that emerge from a deep planning process. Some of those names and faces are also, inevitably, in the senior management team and their direct reports. In this sense, beginning to treat strategy as adaptive work humanizes it, enabling the teams to consider the needs and fears of those who need to be involved in realizing strategic change. This might be an uncomfortable moment, but it can also be relieving or even freeing if you foster curious questions and deep listening.

Map the affected groups and losses for each strategic priority

As part of the implementation phase, develop a different picture or chart with each strategic priority in the center and the most critical groups affected by it. For each group, analyze the extent to which it is necessary for the adaptive challenge to advance, how they contribute, what is essential for them to preserve, and finally, what they will need to leave behind because it is constraining their forward motion. You might not have a complete grasp of what all of these aspects imply.

For example, if one of your strategic priorities is to "accelerate the digital transformation," then write this initiative in the center of the map and recognize five or six fundamental groups or units that will be most affected by the transformation. List for each group the perspective they hold regarding the initiative and the values that underlie that point of view. Then evaluate their commitment and the direct, capability, and loyalty losses they may need to cope with. If you are the senior authority of the organization, don't forget to include yourself on that map. What are the losses you need to acknowledge? What is the learning you need to achieve?

Through the entire process, remain close to people and provide interpersonal support. This does not mean solving people's problems, though you may want to. As a leader, you may be able to solve some of the technical issues that strategic change requires, but the real work is more adaptive. Strategic priorities demand deep systemic and individual learning. Fears must be faced; deep-rooted values will have to be redefined, and behaviors and attitudes will have to change. The basic truth: The people facing the challenge must be part of the solution.

By treating strategic planning as a leadership intervention, you can help people through this process. Adopting an adaptive perspective may not be easy, but ultimately it is more caring and effective.

Natalia Weisz is a professor in organizational behavior at IAE Business School. **Roberto Vassolo** is a professor in strategic management at IAE Business School. They are the coauthors of the book *Strategy as Leadership: Facing Adaptive Challenges in Organizations*.

NOTE

1. Ronald Heifetz, Alexander Grashow, and Martin Linsky, *The Practice of Adaptive Leadership: Tools and Tactics for Changing Your Organization and the World* (Boston: Harvard Business Press, 2009).

Assess Alignment and Capabilities

CHAPTER 7

How Aligned Is Your Organization?

by Jonathan Trevor and Barry Varcoe

Most executives today know their enterprises should be aligned. They know their strategies, organizational capabilities, resources, and management systems should all be arranged to support the enterprise's purpose. The challenge is that executives tend to focus on one of these areas to the exclusion of the others, but what really matters for performance is how they all fit together.

Consider McDonald's. What does it take to be able to serve over 1% of the world's population—more than 70 million customers—every day and in virtually every country across the world? Fanatical attention to the

---

Adapted from content posted on hbr.org, February 7, 2017 (product #H03EMG).

design and management of scalable processes, routines, and a working culture by which simple, stand-alone, and standardized products are sold globally at a predictable, and therefore manageable, volume, quality, and cost. Maximizing economies of scale lies at the heart of McDonald's product-centric business model. Efficiency is built into the design of its winning organization in the form of formalized hierarchies of performance accountability, a high division of labor, routinization of specialist tasks, and teamwork at the point of sale. McDonald's has been the market leader in its sector for decades.

This is what enterprise alignment looks like. It means winning through a tightly managed enterprise value chain that connects an enterprise's *purpose* (what we do and why we do it) to its *business strategy* (what we are trying to win at to fulfill our purpose), *organizational capability* (what we need to be good at to win), *resource architecture* (what makes us good), and, finally, *management systems* (what delivers the winning performance we need). The enterprise value chain is only as strong as its weakest link (see figure 7-1).

Consider the following questions, ideally with your team. You might ask them about the enterprise overall, or about a single strategically important business line, activity, or function.

Enterprise purpose: What do we do and why do we do it?

Purpose is the cornerstone upon which every enterprise is built. Financial success is the consequence of commercial enterprises fulfilling their purposes well, but it is not

FIGURE 7-1

The interdependent components that make up a strategically aligned enterprise

The value chain is only as strong as its weakest link.

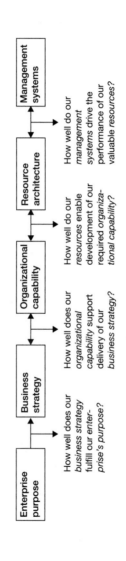

Enterprise purpose	→	Business strategy	→	Organizational capability	→	Resource architecture	→	Management systems

How well does our business strategy fulfill our enterprise's purpose?

How well does our organizational capability support delivery of our business strategy?

How well do our resources enable development of our required organizational capability?

How well do our management systems drive the performance of our valuable resources?

to be confused with enterprise purpose itself. Profit, for example, is rarely a positive focus for people's effort.

Consider your own case: What is the enduring purpose of your enterprise? Why would it matter if you went out of business tomorrow, and who would care? Is your purpose clear enough that your investors, employees, partners, and customers could articulate it?

Business strategy: What are we trying to win at to fulfill our purpose?

If purpose is what the enterprise exists to achieve and why it matters, then business strategy is planning for what the enterprise must win at to fulfill its purpose. Unlike its purpose, an enterprise's strategy should flex and morph in response to future opportunities and threats. The degree to which your enterprise's business strategy fulfills its purpose is the measure of its effectiveness.

The Walt Disney Company's purpose is to "create happiness by providing the finest in entertainment for people of all ages, everywhere."[1] *How* Disney creates happiness is by offering a range of consumer products (Disney Store, publishing, licensing), entertainment (Walt Disney Studios, Pixar, Marvel), and experiences (parks and resorts). It wins by pursuing high performance in each area and by using each to support the others.

Consider the following strategic questions for your own enterprise: What are your offerings to customers in the form of products and services, and are they consistent with your purpose? What's missing? What do you do or offer that you shouldn't? Who are your customers, and what are they demanding of the products and services you offer, now and in the future? Who are your competitors, and what are they capable of offering that you aren't? How do you need to be different to compete and win?

Organizational capability: What do we need to be good at to win?

Business strategy receives the lion's share of executives' attention, but even the best strategy is useless unless supported by appropriate organizational capabilities. It is a reckless leadership team that commits to a business strategy without knowing whether they can achieve it. Traditionally, businesses competed on their ability to execute their planned strategies for matching supply to demand as efficiently as possible. Many enterprises will continue to operate this way in the future, but additional capabilities are increasingly important: the strategic value of organizational capabilities such as agility (around the customer), connectivity (between complementary offerings), and innovativeness (to explore novel opportunities).

Consider your own organizational capabilities: What do you need to be really good at to successfully achieve your winning strategy? What are you capable of organizationally that your rivals are not? How do you become uniquely capable of fulfilling what markets and customers are demanding of you, now and in the future?

Resource architecture: What makes us good? (And how good are we?)

Strategically aligned enterprises are made capable by their organizational resources, including people, structures, cultures, and work processes, and by the degree to which they are configured to be strategically valuable. *People* reflect the value of skills, experience, and knowledge required to perform the enterprise's work; *structure* reflects the value of formal and informal relationships, networks, and functional connections through which work is structured; *processes* reflect the value of planned and ad hoc work processes and routines through which work is performed, and in which valuable knowledge is retained organizationally; and *culture* reflects the values, beliefs, and attitudes that guide everyday working behavior.

Consider your own resources: What type of people are core to you being superior at the things you need to be good at to win? What type of culture might support collaboration between complementary lines of business, if your business strategy depends upon it? What types of work processes are critical to your ability for inventiveness? What type of structure will enable you to be agile enough to compete for and win fickle customers repeatedly?

Management systems: What delivers the winning performance we need?

Management systems include all aspects of management infrastructure, operations, and tactics, from information systems to employee performance management. What management practices, systems, and technologies best fit your winning strategy for fulfilling your enterprise's purpose? What are appropriate measures of success, both short and long term? Where is the focus of effort and attention managerially in your enterprise, and is it aligned to how you plan to win?

Strategically aligned enterprises have a much better chance of winning in today's challenging business environment. To do so, enterprise leaders must find their own distinctive approach to aligning their business strategies, organizational capabilities, valuable resources, and management systems to fulfill their enterprise's purpose.

———————

Jonathan Trevor is an associate professor of management practice at Oxford University's Saïd Business School. **Barry Varcoe** is the global director of real estate and facilities at the Open Society Foundations. Prior to joining the Open Society Foundations, he was an associate fellow at Oxford University's Saïd Business School.

NOTE

1. Disney Institute Team "Customer Service 101: Happiness Is a Purple Balloon," *Disney Institute Blog*, July 13, 2021, https://www.disneyinstitute.com/blog/customer-service-101-happiness-is-a-purple-balloon/.

CHAPTER 8

Design Your Organization to Match Your Strategy

by Ron Carucci and Jarrod Shappell

Strategy execution is commonly fraught with failure. Having worked with hundreds of organizations, we've observed one consistent misstep when leaders attempt to translate strategy into results: the failure to align strategy with the organization's design.

Research suggests that only 10% of organizations are successful at aligning their strategy with their organization design.[1] Some of the problem is a gross misunder-

Adapted from content posted on hbr.org, June 6, 2022 (product #H072AH).

standing of what the word *alignment* actually means in this context. Most leaders naively assume that it means having rigid processes that cascade goals from top to bottom, launching intense communication campaigns that promote top priorities, and shaping budgets to support those priorities. For example, one large manufacturing company we've observed invests countless hours every January having employees input goals that correspond to their boss's goals into their HR system. But employees noted, "It's all cosmetic. We write goals we have no idea if we can achieve, but as long as they appear linked to our boss's goals, they get approved."

The problem is that such processes leave alignment to individuals and ignore the systemic organizational factors needed to make strategy work.

An organization is nothing more than a living embodiment of a strategy. That means its "organizational hardware" (structures, processes, technologies, and governance) and its "organizational software" (values, norms, culture, leadership, and employee skills and aspirations) must be designed exclusively in the service of a specific strategy.

We recently saw this misstep play out with one of our clients—let's call him Ivan—a division president of a technology company. Ivan was presenting his division strategy to the CEO, which included a plan to redesign his organization to align with its new strategy. The CEO curtly asked, "Why do you need to reorg?" Ivan had recently taken over the division, and his predecessor had attempted a botched reorganization, so the CEO was understandably concerned about more churn. Ivan responded, "Well, we have a new set of strategic pillars, including launching a new hardware product bundled with our software. We need an organization design that can deliver."

The CEO's response was telling. He said, "You mean every time we change the strategy, we need to change the organization? Why can't you just force alignment by tying everyone's goals to the same outcomes?"

Unfortunately, it's not that simple. When it comes to executing strategy, alignment means configuring all of the organization's assets in the service of your stated strategy and making sure there is no confusion about what each part of the organization does to bring it to life.

If you're embarking on executing your company's strategy, here are six ways to make sure your organization is designed to do it successfully.

Translate Differentiation into Capabilities

A clear strategy ultimately differentiates you from your competitors. But to ensure that what sets you apart is more than a mere aspiration, you have to build the organizational capabilities needed to actually surpass your competitors.

Know what your current organization is and isn't capable of and what capabilities you need to achieve the newly articulated strategy. Unlike competencies, which belong to individuals, capabilities are organizational. For example, innovation as an organizational capability may result from integrating R&D, consumer analytics, marketing, and product development.

In Ivan's case, he needed to build new capabilities that didn't exist in his division, like product engineering, managing outsourced manufacturing, and new ways of going to market. The existing organization was largely designed to deliver software as a service, and had Ivan attempted to execute his strategy through that design, the new hardware product would have been marginalized.

Every strategy will demand unique competitive capabilities that clearly enable your success. This work that forms these capabilities is work you must be better at than competitors.

Separate Competitive Capabilities from "Everyday Work"

Not all work is equal. True competitive work will get you $5 for every $1 you invest in it. However, "everyday work"—tasks that can be done on par with anyone else or in compliance with regulatory requirements, or even work that adds no value to the final product—must be resourced according to its strategic importance. Problems occur when your competitive and necessary work get too close or intermixed. In other words, the immediacy of everyday tasks takes away from the focus on competitive work.

This is especially challenging when the definitions of "everyday work" and "competitive work" change. In Ivan's case, the role of product engineering had previously been focused solely on ensuring that the division's software could operate on various devices, and the team was buried two levels down within the engineering group. Because the division added its own hardware product, that everyday work became competitive work. To make sure it was competitively resourced, it needed to be elevated to the top of the division, separated from but closely linked to the software products, and staffed with top talent.

Distribute Resources and Decision Rights to the Appropriate Leaders

In the organizations we work with, governance design (which defines who gets to make decisions and allocate resources) is often too complicated or unclear to be effective. For a strategy to be successful, those closest to the most relevant information, budgets, and problems are the best equipped to make decisions. When leaders have proximity to an issue but no authority, authority without the needed resources, or control of the budget but not the people, the decisions tend to follow hierarchical lines. These decisions made at the top may be strategically sound but impossible to implement given how far away they're made from those who must actually execute them.

Ivan recognized that for the division's software and hardware offerings to remain equal in importance and integrated when necessary, he needed a cross-functional team expressly focused on just that. He knew that if everything escalated to his executive team, they would be regularly embroiled in the natural tensions arising from the new organization design.

So, he created a customer success council that included leaders from both product organizations, sales, customer analytics, and those managing the outsourced manufacturing. He empowered them to manage the strategic priorities, trade-offs, and potential conflicts across the organization. This ensured that critical decisions and resources were located with the cross-functional leaders best equipped to make them. This became especially important as salespeople were quickly and successfully selling bundled offerings. Had this team not served as the air-traffic control of the deal flows and prioritization of client resources, it could have been a customer service disaster.

Shut Down Irrelevant Processes and Governance

The new governance is often no match for the legacy behaviors and processes that remain. Like layers of wallpaper in an old house, sometimes you need to strip down to the sheetrock to make way for new decor. Leaders must not only design new governance, but also strip away previous processes and governance that are no longer contributing to the strategy's success.

In Ivan's case, his predecessor had set up several councils that had begun gaining momentum in the service of their old strategy. Those needed to be purged to ensure his new governance design could succeed without confusion or undue conflicts.

Understand Where the Current Culture Will Get in the Way

We've all heard the cliché "culture eats strategy for breakfast," but culture is just one ingredient that enables your strategy's success. Understand the way your thoughts, feelings, and behaviors motivate other leaders to think, feel, and behave in similar ways. And whether you realize it or not, existing values may be rooted in a previous strategy. Consider an organization whose strategy is moving toward increased innovation and has a corporate value of precision. A value like precision could lead to overanalyzing and a low tolerance for risk—the very things needed to encourage a more innovative culture.

Ivan's company emphasized results orientation as a key tenet of its culture, but it often reinforced highly individualistic action at the expense of collaborative work. His new divisional design's success was predicated on a substantial degree of cross-functional collaboration, so his executive team had a spirited debate about how to temper the individualistic interpretation of results orientation to ensure it didn't undermine people's ability to work in teams.

If you want your values to really matter, you must root them in all organizational decisions. For a company's values to feel integral to the lifeblood of the company, they must be visibly central to how the organization competes.

Build Nimble Structures That Allow You to Pivot

Too frequently, leaders assume that a few nips and tucks to the org chart are the equivalent of good design. But those are the Frankenstein "designs" that make people in different parts of the organization feel like they work in different companies. They quickly grow stagnant and are more fit for the PowerPoint slides on which they're loosely drawn than for a dynamic business. For your structure to enable your strategy, it must be agile enough to face the shifts, challenges, and opportunities from its marketplace, stakeholders, and employees.

Nine months into his new design, several of Ivan's strategic partners located in Ukraine were no longer able to provide the technical services they'd long delivered, due to the Russian invasion of the country. Drawing on the expertise of leaders from across the division, the customer success team was able to quickly test and learn where they could make up for that loss of expertise. They identified multiple potential suppliers across the globe and made the decision to better distribute risk by contracting with four of them. Nimble structures allow for readily addressing these unforeseen challenges by making sure that coordination across the organization is easily achieved.

If you want to raise the odds of successfully executing your company's strategy, invest the time in aligning your organization's design to embody the strategy. Instead of relying exclusively on the alignment of goals and metrics, broaden your understanding of alignment to include all the components of your organization. Make sure they fit together congruently into a cohesive organization. You'll signal to your people that you're serious about the strategy and avoid the cynical eye-rolling that often accompanies the announcement of strategies that everyone knows can't be executed.

Ron Carucci is a cofounder and managing partner at Navalent, working with CEOs and executives pursuing transformational change. He is the bestselling author of eight books, including *To Be Honest* and *Rising to Power*. Download his free "How Honest is My Team?" assessment at www.tobehonest.net/assessment. **Jarrod Shappell** is a partner at Navalent who specializes in helping leaders effectively manage themselves by cultivating deeper leadership and relationship skills. He has over 15 years of experience coaching leaders in startup, non-profit, and *Fortune* 500 organizations.

NOTE

1. Trissa Strategy Consulting, "Strategy Execution Statistics: 6 Steps to Successful Strategy Execution," n.d., https://www.trissa consulting.com/articles/strategy-execution-statistics-6-steps-to -successful-strategy-execution.

CHAPTER 9

Capitalizing on Your Capabilities

by Dave Ulrich and Norm Smallwood

If you ask them which companies they admire, people quickly point to organizations like Amazon, Apple, Disney, Microsoft, or Nordstrom. Ask how many layers of management these companies have, though, or how they set strategy, and you'll discover that few know or care. What people respect about the companies is not how they are structured or their specific approaches to management, but their capabilities—an ability to innovate, for example, or to respond with agility to changing market conditions and customer needs. Such *organizational capabilities*, as we call them, are key intangible assets.

Adapted from "Capitalizing on Capabilities," *Harvard Business Review*, June 2004 (product #R0406J).

You can't see or touch them, yet they can make all the difference in the world when it comes to market value.

These capabilities—the collective skills, abilities, and expertise of an organization—are the outcome of investments in staffing, training, compensation, communication, and other human resources areas. They represent the ways that people and resources are brought together to accomplish work. They form the identity and personality of the organization by defining what it is good at doing and, in the end, what it *is known for*. They are stable over time and more difficult for competitors to copy than capital market access, product strategy, or technology. They aren't easy to measure, so managers often pay far less attention to them than to tangible investments like plants and equipment, but these capabilities give investors confidence in future earnings. These intangible assets explain why two firms in the same industry with the same earnings may have dramatically different market value.

In this piece, we look at organizational capabilities and how leaders can evaluate them and build the ones needed to create intangible value. Through case examples, we explain how to do a capabilities audit, which provides a high-level picture of an organization's strengths and areas for improvement. We've conducted and observed dozens of such analyses, and we've found the audit to be a powerful way to evaluate intangible assets and render them concrete and measurable.

Organizational Capabilities Explained

While people often use the words *ability*, *competence*, and *capability* interchangeably, we make some distinc-

FIGURE 9-1

The capability matrix

	Individual	Organizational
Technical	**1** An individual's functional competence	**3** An organization's core competencies
Social	**2** An individual's leadership ability	**4** An organization's capabilities

tions. In technical areas, we refer to an individual's functional competence or an organization's core competencies; on social issues, we refer to an individual's leadership ability or an organization's capabilities. With these differences in mind, let's compare individual and organizational levels of analysis as well as technical and social skill sets, illustrated in figure 9-1.

The individual-technical cell (1) represents a person's functional competence, such as technical expertise in marketing, finance, or manufacturing. The individual-social cell (2) refers to a person's leadership ability—for instance, to set direction, to communicate a vision, or to motivate people. The organizational-technical cell (3) comprises a company's core technical competencies. For example, a financial services firm must know how to manage risk. The organizational-social cell (4) represents an organization's underlying DNA, culture, and personality. These might include such capabilities as innovation, collaboration, and agility.

Organizational capabilities emerge when a company delivers on the combined competencies and abilities of its individuals. An employee may be technically literate or demonstrate leadership skill, but the company as a whole may or may not embody the same strengths. (If it does, employees who excel in these areas will likely be engaged; if not, they may be frustrated.) Additionally, organizational capabilities enable a company to turn its technical know-how into results. A core competence in marketing, for example, won't add value if the organization isn't able to spark change.

There is no magic list of capabilities appropriate to every organization. However, we've identified 11 that well-managed companies tend to have. (Such companies typically excel in as many as three of these areas while maintaining industry parity in the others.) When an organization falls below the norm in any of the 11 capabilities, dysfunction and competitive disadvantage will likely ensue.

Talent

We are good at attracting, motivating, and retaining competent and committed people. Competent employees have the skills for today's and tomorrow's business requirements; committed employees deploy those skills regularly and predictably. Competence comes as leaders *buy* (acquire new talent), *build* (develop existing talent), *borrow* (access thought leaders through alliances or partnerships), *bounce* (remove poor performers), and *bind* (keep the best talent). Leaders can earn commitment from employees by ensuring that the ones who contribute more receive more of what matters to them. Means of assessing this organizational capability include productivity measures, retention statistics (though it's a good sign when employees are targeted by search firms), employee surveys, and direct observation.

Speed or agility

We are good at making important changes rapidly. Speed refers to the organization's ability to recognize opportunities and act with agility, whether to exploit new markets, create new products, establish new employee contracts, or implement new business processes. Speed may be tracked in a variety of ways: how long it takes to go from concept to commercialization, for example, or from the collection of customer data to changes in customer relations. Just as increases in inventory turns show that physical assets are well used, time savings demonstrate improvements in labor productivity as well as increased enthusiasm and responsiveness to opportunities. Leaders should consider creating a return-on-time-invested (ROTI) index so they can monitor the time required for, and the value created by, various activities.

Shared mindset and culture as brand identity

We are good at ensuring that employees and customers have positive and consistent images of and experiences with our organization. Often culture represents internal values, but how much these values are worth to customers becomes a link to brand identity. To gauge shared mindset, ask each member of your team to answer the following question: What are the top three things we want to be known for in the future by our best customers? Measure the degree of consensus by calculating the percent of responses that match one of the three most commonly mentioned items. We have done this exercise hundreds of times, often to find a shared mindset of 50% to 60%; leading companies score in the 80% to 90% range. The next step is to invite key customers to provide feedback on brand identity. The greater the degree of alignment between internal and external mindsets, the greater the value of this capability.

Accountability

We are good at obtaining high performance from employees. Performance accountability becomes an organizational capability when employees realize that failure to meet their goals would be unacceptable to the company. The way to track it is to examine the tools you use to manage performance. By looking at a performance appraisal form, can you derive the strategy of the business? What percent of employees receive an appraisal each year? How much does compensation vary based on employee performance? Some firms claim a pay-for-performance philosophy but give annual compensation increases that range from 3.5% to 4.5%. These companies aren't paying for performance. We would suggest that with an average increase of 4%, an ideal range for acknowledging both low and high performance would be 0% to 12%.

Collaboration

We are good at working across boundaries to ensure both efficiency and leverage. Collaboration occurs when an organization as a whole gains efficiencies of operation through the pooling of services or technologies, through economies of scale, or through the sharing of ideas and talent across boundaries. Sharing services, for example, has been found to produce a savings of 15% to 25% in administrative costs while maintaining acceptable levels of quality. Knowing that the average large company spends about $1,600 per employee per year on administration, you can calculate the probable cost savings of shared services. Collaboration may be tracked both throughout the organization and among teams. You can determine whether your organization is truly collaborative by calculating its breakup value. Estimate what each division of your company might be worth to a potential buyer, then add up these numbers and compare the total with your current market value. As a rule of thumb, if the breakup value is 25% more than the current market value of the assets, collaboration is not one of the company's strengths.

Learning

We are good at generating and generalizing ideas with impact. Organizations generate new ideas through benchmarking (that is, by looking at what other companies are doing), experimentation, competence acquisition (hiring or developing people with new skills and ideas), and continuous improvement. Such ideas are generalized when they move across a boundary of time (from one leader to the next), space (from one geographic location to another), or division (from one structural entity to another). For individuals, learning means letting go of old practices and adopting new ones.

Leadership

We are good at embedding leaders throughout the organization. Companies that consistently produce effective leaders generally have a clear leadership brand—a common understanding of what leaders should know, be, and do. These companies' leaders are easily distinguished from their competitors'. You can track your organization's leadership brand by monitoring the pool of future leaders. How many backups do you have for your top 100 employees? In one company, the substitute-to-star ratio dropped from about 3:1 to about 0.7:1 (less than one qualified backup for each of the top 100 employees) after a restructuring and the elimination of certain development assignments. Seeing the damage to the company's leadership bench, executives encouraged potential leaders to participate in temporary teams, cross-functional assignments, and action-based training activities, thus changing the organization's substitute-to-star ratio to about 1:1.

Customer connectivity

We are good at building enduring relationships of trust with targeted customers. Since it's frequently the case that 20% of customers account for 80% of profits, the ability to connect with targeted customers is a strength. Customer connectivity may come from dedicated account teams, databases that track preferences, or the involvement of customers in HR practices such as staffing, training, and compensation. When a large portion of the employee population has meaningful exposure to or interaction with customers, connectivity is enhanced. To monitor this capability, identify your key accounts and track the share of those important customers over time. Frequent customer-service surveys may also offer insight into how customers perceive your connectivity.

Strategic unity

We are good at articulating and sharing a strategic point of view. Strategic unity is created at three levels: intellectual, behavioral, and procedural. To monitor such unity at the intellectual level, make sure employees from top to bottom know what the strategy is and why it is important. You can reinforce this sort of shared understanding by repeating simple messages; you can measure it by noting how consistently employees respond when asked about the company's strategy. To gauge strategic accord at the behavioral level, ask employees how much of their time is spent in support of the strategy and whether their suggestions for improvement are heard and acted on. When it comes to process, continually invest in procedures that are essential to your strategy.

Innovation

We are good at doing something new in both content and process. Innovation—whether in products, administrative processes, business strategies, channel strategies, geographic reach, brand identity, or customer service—focuses on the future rather than on past successes. It excites employees, delights customers, and builds confidence among investors. This capability may be tracked through a vitality index (for instance, one that records revenues or profits from products or services created in the last three years).

Efficiency

We are good at managing costs. While it's not possible to save your way to prosperity, leaders who fail to manage costs will not likely have the opportunity to grow the top line. Efficiency may be the easiest capability to track. Inventories, direct and indirect labor, capital employed, and costs of goods sold can all be viewed on balance sheets and income statements.

Conducting a Capabilities Audit

Just as a financial audit tracks cash flow and a 360-degree review assesses leadership behaviors, a capabilities audit can help you monitor your company's intangible assets. It will highlight which ones are most important given the company's history and strategy, measure how well the company delivers on these capabilities, and lead to an action plan for improvement. This exercise can work for an entire organization, a business unit, or a region. Indeed, any part of a company that has a strategy for producing financial or customer-related results can do an audit, as long as it has the backing of the leadership team. We'll walk through the process below, describing as we go the experiences of two companies that performed such audits—Boston Scientific (a medical device manufacturer) and InterContinental Hotels Group—and what they did as a result of their findings.

We'll start with Boston Scientific, which wanted to engage the leadership team in a capabilities audit to improve the international division's success. The first step was to identify the areas that were critical in meeting the group's goals. Using the 11 generic capabilities we've defined as a starting point, leaders at Boston Scientific adapted the language to suit their business requirements. (No matter how you create the list, the capabilities you audit should reflect those needed to deliver on your company's strategic promises.) Next, to evaluate the organization's performance on these capabilities, the international division's executives—along with their bosses and employees and a group of peer executives from other divisions—completed a short online survey. Adapted from the generic questionnaire shown in table 9-1, "How to perform a capabilities audit," the survey comprised 20 questions, with space for comments. For each capability, respondents were asked to rate on a scale of one to five the group's current performance as well as the level of achievement the division would need to meet its goals. This exercise showed gaps between current and desired capability. For example, on strategic unity—the extent to which employees understood and agreed upon strategy—the score for actual achievement was 0.91 points lower than the score for desired performance. Respondents also chose two capabilities that would most affect the group's ability to deliver on its customer-related and financial promises.

The leaders discussed the survey findings at an off-site meeting. To address the strategic-unity gap, they developed a clearer statement of strategy that sharpened the group's focus on service and profitability. Then, before forming an overall improvement plan, they defined the

TABLE 9-1

How to perform a capabilities audit

A capabilities audit will help you gauge—and ultimately boost—your organization's intangible value. First, select a business unit (plant, division, region, zone, industry). Then, using the following questions as a guide— and keeping in mind your overall business strategy—assess the unit's performance in each organizational capability (0=worst; 10=best), and rank the capabilities in terms of improvement needed (1=highest priority, 2=next highest, and so on).

Organizational capabilities	Questions	Assessments	Rankings
Talent	Do our employees have the competencies and the commitment required to deliver the business strategy in question?		
Speed	Can we move quickly to make important things happen fast?		
Shared mindset and coherent brand identity	Do we have a culture or identity that reflects what we stand for and how we work? Is it shared by both customers and employees?		
Accountability	Does high performance matter to the extent that we can ensure execution of strategy?		
Collaboration	How well do we collaborate to gain both efficiency and leverage?		
Learning	Are we good at generating new ideas with impact and generalizing those ideas across boundaries?		
Leadership	Do we have a leadership brand that directs managers on which results to deliver and how to deliver them?		
Customer connectivity	Do we form enduring relationships of trust with targeted customers?		
Strategic unity	Do our employees share an intellectual, behavioral, and procedural agenda for our strategy?		
Innovation	How well do we innovate in product, strategy, channel, service, and administration?		
Efficiency	Do we reduce costs by closely managing processes, people, and projects?		

capabilities that would be most critical to executing that strategy. They didn't necessarily choose capabilities with low scores in actual performance. For example, even though the group showed relative weakness in learning and innovation, the leadership team didn't see those capabilities as essential to meeting group goals, because the division is primarily a sales, marketing, and distribution arm of the company. However, although the division scored high on talent (see the sidebar "Does the Talent Deliver?"), the leaders chose to invest in further developing this capability since it would be critical to success; in particular, they focused on strengthening marketing skills and building talent that would allow them to target a broader set of customers. They also launched an effort to create a leadership brand, starting with a new model of high performance. Finally, they began to assess bench strength in support of that leadership brand, starting with the organization's three regional presidents.

The idea, in short, is not necessarily to boost weak capabilities but to identify and build capabilities that will have the strongest and most direct impact on the execution of strategy.

The Berkshire, England–based InterContinental Hotels Group (IHG) conducted its audit across the entire company in an effort to improve performance. As at Boston Scientific International, the audit process started with collection of feedback from multiple sources—executives, employees at all levels, and franchisees who owned and managed individual hotels. The information was gathered by an organization-review design team made up of high-potential employees from all regions.

DOES THE TALENT DELIVER?

In an online survey designed to gauge their division's capabilities, executives at Boston Scientific International asked respondents to answer the following question on a scale of one to five, with one meaning "not at all" and five meaning "absolutely": Do international leaders ensure that they have the best talent required to accomplish their strategy? The responses were positive but nonetheless indicated room for improvement in this key area.

This exercise made the intangible strengths and weaknesses of the international group tangible. It compared how executives from different parts of Boston Scientific—inside and outside the international group—viewed the division's capabilities, and it provided a baseline score against which to measure the impact of future investments in these capabilities. Leaders then planned to revisit the effort in a year to learn whether their investments had made a difference.

FIGURE 9-2

Respondents		Talent scores
Executive committee		4.00
Operations committee		3.50
Senior marketing leaders		4.00
International senior staff		4.60
Other functional leaders		3.67
Average score		**3.95**

Supported by external consultants, the team members worked on the review process full-time for several months before making recommendations to the IHG executive committee. Based on this review, efficiency, or reducing costs, quickly became a priority. The company's costs were 15% to 20% higher than the industry average, and IHG swiftly took measures to streamline its operations among the various regions, creating a shared services center and aligning finance, human resources, and corporate functions.

IHG executives also looked at what capabilities would be essential for future success, assessing actual and desired capabilities in terms of where the company required world-class skill, where it needed to demonstrate industry superiority, and where it needed to achieve industry parity for optimal cost-efficiency. (For a visual breakdown of the areas examined, see figure 9-3, "A snapshot of IHG's capabilities audit results.") The capabilities under review supported the overarching priority of efficiency. Leaders decided, for example, that the company should achieve world-class performance in collaboration. As part of this strategic push, IHG gave up its decentralized structure, in which each region operated independently and was responsible for its own budget and operation, and became a unified corporate entity whose regions needed to work together to solve budget shortfalls, information technology challenges, and the like. By collaborating across regions and hotels, IHG streamlined operations and saved more than $100 million a year. By focusing on the gap between actual and desired capabilities, company leaders were able to determine where to invest leadership attention.

FIGURE 9-3

A snapshot of IHG's capabilities audit results

InterContinental Hotels Group executives chose which capabilities would be most essential to the company's future success and then collected feedback on how well IHG delivered on these capabilities. The accompanying chart shows both actual and desired levels of accomplishment. In the capabilities designated critical for world-class success, IHG needed to invest fairly significantly in improvements. In the areas that demanded superior performance, it needed to invest, but not as heavily. And when it came to the capabilities where IHG needed to be on par, the company was already on-target and could thus focus on efficiency and cost reduction.

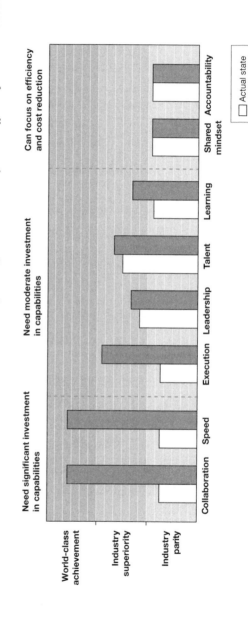

In the past couple of years, we have developed another audit tool—the Organization Guidance System (OGS). OGS is unique in that it does not just examine how well a company delivers a capability compared with others. The OGS identifies which capabilities most impact a targeted stakeholder result (employee, strategy, customer, investor, or community). For example, if an organization wants to improve financial results, which of the 11 capabilities matters most? The OGS delivers a unique report to an organization determined by statistical factors such as how well the organization currently performs the capability, the variance for each dimension, and the impact of a dimension on the business outcomes. Figure 9-4 is a sample report showing the overall results.

Lessons Learned

No two audits will look exactly the same, but our experience has shown us that, in general, there are good and bad ways to approach the process. You'll be on the right track if you observe a few guidelines.

Get focused

It's better to excel at a few targeted capabilities than to diffuse leadership energy over many. Leaders should choose no more than three on which to spend their time and attention; they should aim to make at least two of them world-class. This means identifying which capabilities will have the most impact and will be easiest to implement, and prioritizing accordingly. (Boston Scientific chose talent, leadership, and speed. IHG zeroed in on collaboration and speed since the company's leaders

FIGURE 9-4

Global organization capability OGS results

In this example, if financial results are desired, the biggest impact is found by focusing on the strategic clarity capability—the only cell shaded dark grey in the financial column. Alternatively, if employee results are desired, there are more options, such as building talent, increasing agility, and improving customer centricity.

WHAT GUIDANCE CAN WE OFFER?

ORGANIZATION CAPABILITIES	Employee	Strategy/Business	Customer	Financial	Social citizenship
Talent					
Agility					
Strategic clarity					
Customer centricity					
Culture					
Collaboration					
Social responsibility					
Innovation					
Efficiency					
Accountability					
Information					
Leveraging technology					

Low Impact   Medium Impact   High Impact

felt that working across boundaries faster would enable them to reach their strategic and financial goals.) The remaining capabilities identified in the audit should meet standards of industry parity. Investors seldom seek assurance that an organization is average or slightly above average in every area; rather, they want the organization to have a distinct identity that aligns with its strategy.

Recognize the interdependence of capabilities

While you need to be focused, it's important to understand that capabilities depend on one another. So even though you should target no more than three for primary attention, the most important ones often need to be combined. For example, speed won't be enough on its own; you will likely need fast learning, fast innovation, or fast collaboration. As any capability improves, it will probably improve others in turn. We assume that no capabilities are built without leaders, so working on any one of them builds leadership. As the quality of leadership improves, talent and collaboration issues often surface—and in the process of resolving those problems, the company usually strengthens its accountability and learning.

Learn from the best

Compare your organization with companies that have world-class performance in your target capabilities. Quite possibly, these companies won't be in the same industry as your organization. It's often helpful, therefore, to look for analogous industries where companies may have developed extraordinary strength in the capability you desire. For example, hotels and airlines have many differences, but they're comparable when it comes to

STEP-BY-STEP THROUGH THE AUDIT PROCESS

While the particulars of a capabilities audit will differ from company to company, leaders should follow these five basic steps:

1. **Determine which part of the business to audit.** This can be a division, a region, the entire company—any unit responsible for delivering on a strategy.

2. **Create the content of the audit.** Adapt the 11 generic capabilities outlined in this piece to the organization's requirements. (You may want to add "quality," for example.) A tailor-made audit template will yield the most-precise information.

3. **Gather data from multiple groups on current and desired capabilities.** This information may be collected by degrees.

   - For a 90-degree assessment, collect data only from the leadership team of the unit being audited. This method is quick but often deceptive, as the leaders' self-reports may be biased.

   - For a 360-degree assessment, collect data from multiple groups within the company. Different groups may tell very different stories, as happened at Boston Scientific International, and can provide insights that might otherwise be missed.

STEP-BY-STEP THROUGH THE AUDIT PROCESS

- For a 720-degree assessment, collect information not only from inside the company but from outside groups. External assessors might include investors, customers, or suppliers. These groups are important because it is in their eyes that the organization's intangible value matters most. InterContinental Hotels Group did a 720-degree assessment to some extent by including franchisees in its data sample.

4. **Synthesize the data to identify the most critical capabilities requiring managerial attention.** Look for patterns in the data and focus leadership attention on no more than three capabilities required to deliver on strategy goals. You'll need to identify which capabilities will have the most impact and which will be the easiest to improve.

5. **Put together an action plan with clear steps to take and measures to monitor, and assign a team to the job of delivering on the critical capabilities.** Actions might include coordinating education or training events, setting performance standards, creating task forces or other organizational units to house those doing the work, or investing in technology to sustain the capability. Establish a time frame of 90 days for the plan's execution.

several driving forces: stretching capital assets, pleasing travelers, employing direct-service workers, and so on. The advantage of looking outside your own industry for models is that you can emulate them without competing with them. They're far more likely than your top competitors to share insights with you.

Create a virtuous cycle of assessment and investment

A rigorous assessment helps company executives figure out what capabilities will be required for success, so they can in turn decide where to invest. Over time, repetitions of the assessment-investment cycle result in a baseline that can be useful for benchmarking.

Compare capability perceptions

Like 360-degree feedback in leadership assessments, capabilities audits sometimes reveal differing views of the organization. For example, employees or customers may not agree with top leaders' perception that there is a shared mindset. Involve stakeholders in improvement plans. If investors rank the firm low on various capabilities, for instance, the CEO or CFO might want to meet with the investors to discuss specific action plans for moving forward.

Match capability with delivery

Leaders need to do more than talk about capability; they need to demonstrate it. Rhetoric shouldn't exceed action. Expectations for improvement should be outlined in a detailed plan. One approach is to bring together leaders for a half-day session to generate questions for the plan to address: What measurable outcome do we want to accomplish with this capability? Who is responsible for delivering on it? How will we monitor our progress in attaining or boosting this capability? What decisions can we make immediately to foster improvement? What actions can we as leaders take to promote this capability? Such actions may include developing education or training programs, designing new systems for performance management, and implementing structural changes to house the needed capabilities. The best capability plans specify actions and results that will occur within a 90-day window. HR professionals may be the architects, but managers are responsible for executing these plans.

Avoid underinvestment in organization intangibles

Often, leaders fall into the trap of focusing on what is easy to measure instead of what is in greatest need of repair. They read balance sheets that report earnings, EVA, or other economic data but miss the underlying organizational factors that may add value. At times the capability goals can be very concrete, as with IHG's focus on efficiency.

Don't confuse capabilities with activities

An organizational capability emerges from a bundle of activities, not any single pursuit. So leadership training, for instance, needs to be understood in terms of the capability to which it contributes, not just the activity that takes place. Instead of asking what percent of leaders received 40 hours of training, ask what capabilities the leadership training created. To build speed, IHG leaders made changes in the company's structure, budgeting processes, compensation system, and other management practices. Attending to capabilities helps leaders avoid looking for single, simple solutions to complex business problems.

Few would dispute that intangible assets matter. But it can be quite difficult to measure them and even harder to communicate their value to stakeholders. An audit is a way of making capabilities visible and meaningful. It helps executives assess company strengths and weaknesses, assists senior leaders in defining strategy, supports midlevel managers in executing strategy, and enables frontline leaders to make things happen. And it helps customers, investors, and employees alike recognize the organization's intangible value.

———————

Dave Ulrich is the Rensis Likert Professor of Business at the Ross School, University of Michigan, and a partner at the RBL Group. He studies how organizations build capabilities of leadership, speed, learning, accountability, and talent through human resources. **Norm Smallwood** is a cofounder of the RBL Group, a strategic HR and leadership systems advisory firm, and the coauthor of several books, including *Agile Talent* (Harvard Business Review Press, 2016). He is a partner in the Agile Talent Collaborative.

CHAPTER 10

The Problem with Learning Is Unlearning

by Mark Bonchek

Ever since the publication of Peter Senge's *The Fifth Discipline* 25 years ago, companies have sought to become "learning organizations" that continually transform themselves. In our era of digital disruption, this goal is more important than ever. But even the best companies still struggle to make real progress in this area.

One problem is that they've been focused on the wrong thing. The problem isn't learning: It's *unlearning*. In every aspect of business, we are operating with

---

Adapted from "Why the Problem with Learning Is Unlearning," on hbr.org, November 3, 2016 (product #H038PP).

mental models that have grown outdated or obsolete, from strategy to marketing to organization to leadership. To embrace the new logic of value creation, we have to unlearn the old one.

Unlearning is not about forgetting. It's about the ability to choose an alternative mental model or paradigm. When we learn, we add new skills or knowledge to what we already know. When we unlearn, we step outside the mental model in order to choose a different one.

As an example, last summer I rented a car to travel around Great Britain. I had never driven this kind of car before, so I had to learn the placement of the various controls. I also had to learn how to drive on the left side of the road. All of that was relatively easy. The hard part was *unlearning* how to drive on the right. I had to keep telling myself to "stay left." It's the reason crosswalks in London have reminders for pedestrians to "look right." It's not easy to unlearn the mental habits that no longer serve us.

The same thing happens in business. Many of the paradigms we learned in school and built our careers on are either incomplete or ineffective.

In strategy, an entire generation grew up with Michael Porter's five forces. In this model, competitive advantage is achieved by driving costs down, driving prices up, locking in customers, and locking out competitors and entrants. In Porter's view, "the essence of strategy is that you must set limits on what you're trying to accomplish."[1]

But in a networked economy, the nature of strategy, value creation, and competitive advantage change from incremental to exponential. Companies like Apple and

Amazon achieve exponential results by focusing on how to remove limits rather than set them. They look beyond controlling the pipe that delivers a product and instead build platforms that enable others to create value. They look to create network effects through ecosystems of customers, suppliers, and partners.

The Porter model of strategy isn't obsolete. But it is decidedly incomplete. It takes unlearning to see the model as only one possibility rather than canonical truth. As the saying goes, "The map is not the territory."

In the field of marketing, our thinking is permeated by the mental model of mass communication. The world has become many-to-many, but we still operate with a one-to-many mindset. Everything is linear and transactional. We segment into discrete buckets even though people are multidimensional. We treat customers as consumers even when they want to be cocreators. We target buyers and run campaigns that push messages through channels even though real engagement increasingly happens through shared experiences. We move people through a pipeline that goes in one direction even though the customer journey is nonlinear.

We need to unlearn the push model of marketing and explore alternative models. For example, instead of using relationships to drive transactions, we could be building brand orbits and embedding transactions in relationships. Instead of customers being consumers, we could have relationships with them in a variety of roles and social facets. Beyond delivering a value proposition, we could be fulfilling a shared purpose.

The process of unlearning has three parts.

- **First, you have to recognize that the old mental model is no longer relevant or effective.** This is a challenge because we are usually unconscious of our mental models. They are the proverbial water to the fish. In addition, we might be afraid to admit that the existing model is growing outdated. We have built our reputations and careers on the mastery of these old models. Letting go can seem like starting over and losing our status, authority, or sense of self.

- **Second, you need to find or create a new model that can better achieve your goals.** At first, you will probably see this new model through the lens of the old. Many companies are ineffective in their use of social media because they still think of it as a channel for distributing a message. They haven't made the mental shift from one-to-many to many-to-many. Social is best thought of as a context rather than a channel.

- **Third, you need to ingrain the new mental habits.** This process is no different from creating a new behavioral habit, like your diet or golf swing. The tendency will be to fall back into the old way of thinking and therefore the old way of doing. It's useful to create signals that alert you to which model you are working from. For example, when you are talking about your customers, catch yourself when you call them "consumers"—this corresponds to a transactional mindset. Find a word that reflects a more collaborative relationship. The shift in language helps to reinforce the shift in mindset.

The good news is that practicing unlearning will make it easier and quicker to make the shifts as your brain adapts. (It's a process called neuroplasticity.) As you begin unlearning, be patient with yourself—it's not a linear process.

Albert Einstein once said, "We cannot solve our problems with the same thinking we used when we created them." In this time of transformative change, we need to be conscious of our mental models and ambidextrous in our thinking. Sometimes the incremental models of barriers to entry, linear campaigns, and hierarchical controls will be the right ones. But we need to unlearn these models and replace them with exponential models based on network effects, brand orbits, and distributed networks. The place to start is by unlearning how we think about learning.

Mark Bonchek is the creator of Shift Thinking and the founder of Epiphany Labs. Mark has been a pioneer on the digital frontier since his doctoral thesis predicted social media in 1997. He works with leaders and organizations to design better thinking for a better world.

NOTE

1. Keith H. Hammonds, "Michael Porter's Big Ideas," *Fast Company*, February 28, 2001, https://www.fastcompany.com/42485/michael-porters-big-ideas.

Communicate Clearly

CHAPTER 11

How to Communicate Your Company's Strategy Effectively

by David Lancefield

Most people can't recall the strategy of the organization they work for. Even the executives and managers responsible for strategy struggle, with one study reporting that only 28% of them could list three strategic priorities.[1]

It's not surprising. Many organizations don't have a strategy. The few that do find it hard to communicate effectively, as it requires engaging with a wide range of stakeholders in different situations. They find it easier

---

Adapted from content posted on hbr.org, November 29, 2022 (product #H07CQW).

and less risky to issue lofty purpose statements, describe big goals, launch initiatives, or publish fixed plans instead.

Communicating strategy clearly increases the chances of an organization "winning" by helping people decide where to focus their attention, energy, resources, and capabilities. Unclear communication results in wasted effort from lack of alignment and confusion, which leads to inertia.

If you're embarking on communicating your organization's strategy, here are five ways to do it clearly.

Communicate Comprehensively

Communications sometimes focus on one aspect of strategy to the detriment of others. For example, they lay out how to beat the competition but forget to address how best to serve customers. Or they describe an exciting vision but leave out important details of how the organization will deliver on it. They outline the trends, dynamics, and disruptions but fail to clearly articulate the choices they've made to address them.

The same goes for the audience. Executives prioritize communicating with employees and investors and then forget to engage with wider stakeholders, such as regulators or community groups, until they raise questions or objections.

To combat this narrow focus, a chief of staff I worked with developed a central repository of answers to frequently asked questions about her company's strategy and highlighted the most important ones for each stakeholder group. This better prepared her to customize the message for the audience, which increased the efficacy of the communications. She also invited colleagues to contribute. That improved not just the quality of the answers but also the consistency of messages across the organization, as those contributors felt a greater sense of ownership.

To communicate strategy comprehensively, you'll need to:

- **Visualize your ambition.** To create intrigue, spark imagination, and build excitement in a better future, focus attention on the opportunities and possibilities ahead. ("At our best we will become . . . ")

- **Describe the contribution you want to make.** Articulate the impact of the strategy on customers, wider stakeholders (for example, citizens), and systems (for example, the environment). ("We will make a significant contribution to our shareholders and the society we operate in by . . . ")

- **Challenge the status quo.** Encourage people to see the merits in trying a new path, overcoming personal and organizational inertia. ("We're not serving our customers as best we can because . . . ")

- **Instill belief in the organization.** Signal confidence in the organization's ability to get there while acknowledging there will be some changes. ("We've shown what we're capable of before when we've applied the right mindset . . . ")

- **Focus attention on what matters.** Give people the opportunity to make the decisions they're most capable of making about where to focus their time in line with the strategy—a process author Roger Martin calls "strategic choice chartering."[2] ("In my business area, we've chosen to focus on serving [x] customers in [these geographies] because [y] and we'll win by being the best at [z]. The next choice is how and where to . . . ")

- **Outline what will change.** Encourage people to start making changes to the way they work. ("To deliver on the strategy, we'll need to invest in these capabilities, deploy resources in new areas, and change the way we work.")

- **Set out the metrics.** Clarify the behaviors, activities, and outcomes that are central to the strategy and assign metrics to them. ("We will measure our success in delivering on this strategy by the following metrics at the organizational and individual levels.")

- **Explain the thinking, logic, and evidence that supports the choices.** Build credibility and confidence in the ambition, choices, and investments. ("This strategy is based on a number of important data points and assumptions.")

- **Describe the process.** Instill confidence in the way you've developed the strategy. ("We developed this strategy in open dialogue throughout the process, inviting ideas and suggestions.")

In most cases it's not necessary to do this in one go. The trick is to combine the right message with the audience using the most effective medium, listening attentively to the responses and contributions, and refining the communication (if not aspects of the strategy) as required.

Make It Personal

Communications often paint a corporate picture of the world that doesn't actually convey what's expected of the audience—or how it benefits them.

Steve, a CEO I worked with, walked offstage feeling great after presenting the new strategy to his team. The rehearsals he did had paid off. He landed all the important points and effectively included personal anecdotes and humor. Or so he thought.

As the audience members shared their reactions with me, I could see that they were less convinced: "That was some performance"; "It's clear what the future looks like. But I have no idea what it means for me. What should I change? How will I change?"; "How will this strategy help my career?"; "The other executive committee members were nodding, but are they truly on board?"

Take four actions to avoid this scenario:

- Show that you're implementing the strategy yourself through the choices you make. Prioritize spending your time, attention, and energy on the activities that best enable the strategy. Talk through areas of confusion or disagreement in your team to build alignment and commitment. Reflect on how your decisions and words are consistent with the strategy.

- Describe the new activities, capabilities, and behaviors that enable the strategy, and establish pilots to start rolling them out.

- Tackle nostalgia, fears, or frictions that might hold people back, such as, "We've tried this before and it didn't work, so what's different this time?" or "How can we improve our speed to market when we have to wade through so much bureaucracy?"

- Help people upskill—for example, through training programs (which should include teaching people about strategy, not just their functional skill sets), coaching, or mentoring.

Match the Message to the Moment

Communicating strategy often involves long, bombastic slide presentations or brief, bland statements online. By themselves, these rarely create the excitement, engagement, advocacy, or recall required to effect change.

Instead, design your communication as a series of engaging and dynamic exercises—with an emphasis on brevity and clarity. This requires three steps:

- **Map out the critical or "imprintable" moments— including the people involved—where you want to communicate strategy.** This could be an interview with a recruit, a pitch to investors, a board meeting, a town hall presentation, a team huddle, or a performance appraisal.

- **Decide what messages you want to emphasize.** If you're with a potential partner organization, you might want to focus on the ambition and opportunity ahead, whereas with a group of managers, you'll want to articulate the choices and changes you've made and encourage them to make their own.

- **Select the tool or asset that best works for the people, moment, and message.** For a one-on-one conversation, you might use a two-minute (or even shorter) elevator pitch or an anecdote about the organization's advantage. In a larger group setting, a visualization that describes elements of the strategy, or a story that illustrates how the organization will overcome the challenges it faces, works well. In an email, you might use a one-paragraph summary of the strategy, along with some answers to frequently asked questions, and a personal reflection on what it means to you.

As an example of online communication, telecommunications company BT uses a single visual on its website to connect purpose, ambition, values, and strategy. British Petroleum set out its strategic narrative in a well-written press release, while carmaker Renault presented its "Renaulation" plan in a highly visual, content-rich presentation.

Empower People Through Transparency

The responsibility for communicating strategy is often restricted to a select few, based on two mistaken beliefs: Only the top team has responsibility for strategy, and strategy is too complex for others to communicate.

Information is also restricted based on two other mistaken beliefs: Too much detail will distract people, and competitors will gain an advantage from knowing more about the strategy.

This approach limits the opportunity for employees, partners, suppliers, and other stakeholders to contribute to, advocate for, and deliver on the strategy. They want to hear from people they work closely with—not just the top team—and to understand the full picture.

One CFO I worked with made a point to explain on calls and in meetings how what she and her team were doing contributed to the strategy. She also encouraged people involved in the development of strategy to play a prominent role in the program of communications and to act as advocates in their daily activities. This ranged from people who contributed ideas and perspectives in crowdsourcing events to those who played a central role in designing the strategy (including representatives from corporate development, sales, customer service, operations, and HR).

Help people understand the strategy and make their own choices by:

- **Sharing as much of the strategy as possible**, explaining the critical decisions, assumptions made, and uncertainties. Provide the assets and information in one place so that people can select what they're interested in.

- **Describing how important decisions enable the strategy**, such as a new investment, closure, restructure, or partnership.

- **Communicating progress honestly.** Share updates on what's working and what's challenging and invite people to contribute ideas.

- **Holding back detail wisely.** Only restrict information if it has the potential to overwhelm or confuse people or undermine commercial activity (for example, a potential acquisition or new venture).

- **Creating open channels.** Make it easy for people to share ideas, raise challenges, and ask questions.

Repeat, Listen, and Refresh

After the launch of a strategy, life often goes back to "normal" as people revert to old habits, practices, and routines, especially in many large, traditional companies. Communications fade away. Apart from the wasted effort, it leaves the organization less resilient and more susceptible to disruption.

Strategy needs to evolve in a world that is more volatile and uncertain than before. Its communication, therefore, needs to be both systematic and flexible. This requires you to:

- **Map out clear sequences of communications.** Involve different stakeholder groups in different moments to ensure clarity and consistency of messages. Research suggests it takes about two months to embed a new habit, even with the best communications and incentives—so this needs to be a sustained effort and include some repetition.[3] You'll know it's resonating when stakeholders start to use the same language and, most important, start making their own choices about where to focus and how to work differently.

- **Ask questions to encourage participation and overcome obstacles.** Think, "What can we do to accelerate the changes?" or "What can we remove to make our lives easier?" Listen carefully to the answers.

- **Monitor weak signals of change.** Look both within and outside the organization for anything that should change the content and nature of communication (let alone the strategy). For example, if there's a change in consumer sentiment or aggressive competitor activity, communications should call out the resilience of the strategy (or the reasons for changes).

- **Surface and highlight success stories.** Doing so reinforces the messages, maintains interest, and builds commitment.

For too long, communicating strategy has been an afterthought. Executives have shared long, bombastic documents or withheld critical information and expected people to just "get it." And it hasn't worked. Greater external uncertainty, collaboration, employee anxiety, and organizational openness demands a change of approach. These five actions will improve the clarity and quality of communication, enabling people to make a more substantive and meaningful contribution to the strategy.

David Lancefield is a catalyst, strategist, and coach for leaders. He's advised more than 40 CEOs and hundreds of executives, was a senior partner at Strategy&, and is a guest lecturer at the London Business School. Find him on LinkedIn @davidclancefield or at davidlancefield.com, where you can sign up for his free "Mastering Big Moments" workbook.

NOTES

1. Donald Sull, Charles Sull, and James Yoder, "No One Knows Your Strategy—Not Even Your Top Leaders," *MIT Sloan Management Review*, February 12, 2018, https://sloanreview.mit.edu/article/no-one-knows-your-strategy-not-even-your-top-leaders/.

2. Roger Martin, "Strategic Choice Chartering," *Roger Martin* (blog), November 9, 2020, https://rogermartin.medium.com/strategic-choice-chartering-3d56d8962ec3.

3. James Clear, "How Long Does It Actually Take to Form a New Habit? (Backed by Science)," *James Clea* (blog), n.d., https://jamesclear.com/new-habit.

CHAPTER 12

Good Leadership Is About Communicating "Why"

by Nancy Duarte

At my company, we rework thousands of talks each year for large brands and high-powered executives. When their communications are high stakes, most of our clients come to us prepared with *what* needs to happen and *how*. But they've rarely answered one essential question: *Why?*

Adapted from content posted on hbr.org, May 6, 2020 (product #H05LAY).

So, *why* answer *why*?

Let's put it this way: If your boss comes to you and says, "I need you to take on this additional project on top of your current workload," what is your first question going to be? It probably has nothing to do with setting your alarm, rearranging your schedule, or any other version of *how* you're going to get the extra work done. When someone asks you to alter a current behavior, your first question is usually *"Why?"* because you're not going to try something new or hard unless you're *motivated* to do so.

Your audience is no different. If they don't know *why* a new action is necessary, they won't be motivated to help you. They'll continue with their current comfortable behaviors, thank you very much.

Communicators often overlook answering *why* for two key reasons:

- They assume explaining *what* and *how* is the fastest way to influence their audience.

- They think the answer to *why* is so self-evident, it doesn't need unpacking.

Think about a difficult situation where it's critical for people to rally and align. Something as simple as a team-defining internal initiative or something as grand as pulling out of an economic crisis through a new organizational strategy. Let's say you are confident that if your audience executes your plan, your company will pull out unscathed. You know how to do it. You pour all those insights into a passionate presentation. You get a smattering of applause and then . . . nothing happens.

Have you been there? You've worked through your scenarios, planning, research, and validation and poured energy into communicating what needs to happen and how to do it. You've walked away disappointed by the lack of response from the very people whose lives will be improved if they would simply do what you said how you said to do it.

Let's dissect this example a bit more.

Leaders explain the *what* of their insights and the *how* of applying the findings. This is how most leaders approach their talks, especially professionals who are deep subject-matter experts. They focus on the content they want to share. Many leaders don't even consider the *why* from the audience perspective because it seems so self-evident to them, they think it's obvious to everyone.

On the other hand, let's say you inject your talk with a compelling *why*—"We can reduce secondary infection rates by 40%, saving thousands of lives" or "We can reach more people and help them advance their careers if we release our content for free." Answering why often leads to a human who will benefit from the action you're asking people to take. It suddenly matters.

There's a good chance your *why* won't be as clear-cut as these examples. So here are three strategies to help you get to the heart of the *why* in your next communication.

Ask Some Good *What* Questions

The answers to *why* often hide in our subconscious, and you may have to coax them out. Sometimes, you can get to *why* by asking yourself a few good *what* questions such as:

- What is at stake if we do or do not do this?

- What will the future look like if we get this done?

- What would the state of the human condition be if we did or didn't do this?

Another way to get to *why* is to have someone else ask you, "So what?" until you can't answer it anymore. That'll get you to the root of *why*.

Follow Up with *Because*

Just considering the *why* isn't enough—you have to clearly articulate it. Think about what action you're asking your audience to take, and then follow it with "because."

For example, "We need to improve our process, because _____." Whatever reason follows a "we need to _____, because _____ ." Whatever that second blank is will answer the question of *why*.

State Alternate Perspectives

Address skeptics and resistance by mentioning potential perspectives you've eliminated. It might sound counter-intuitive to reveal anything *other* than the action you're influencing them to take, but you can better persuade an audience by sharing ideas you abandoned and—you guessed it—why you've eliminated them. By stating the options that you considered, explored, tested, and then abandoned, you'll demonstrate that you've thought through all the possibilities.

Answering *why* is an act of empathy and adds a layer of persuasion to your communications. When people know *why* they're being asked to do something, they're much more likely to do it.

Nancy Duarte is a bestselling author with 30 years of CEO-ing under her belt. She's driven her firm, Duarte, Inc., to be the global leader behind some of the most influential messages and visuals in business and culture. Duarte, Inc., is the largest design firm in Silicon Valley, as well as one of the top woman-owned businesses in the area. Nancy has written six bestselling books, and four have won awards. She is the author of the *HBR Guide to Persuasive Presentations*, and her latest book is *DataStory: Explain Data and Inspire Action Through Story*. Follow her on Twitter @nancyduarte.

CHAPTER 13

Be Aware of the Signals You're Sending

by Elsbeth Johnson

A former colleague liked to remind leaders of their impact by telling them, "There are children you've never met who know your name." The point was simple: Many of their followers were also parents who were going home and talking about their day in front of their children. And you, their leader, had a starring role in that story. As leaders, we are far more visible than we realize, and we are sending signals to followers all the time—even when we don't realize it.

Adapted from "How to Communicate Clearly During Organizational Change," on hbr.org, June 13, 2017 (product #H03PQF).

And while sending the right signals to our followers is important at any time, it is especially important during times of strategic change, when followers are trying to make sense of a new "ask" from the organization, in the context of all the existing asks they are grappling with.

Why, then, is it so hard for leaders to send clear, effective signals to followers?

In my experience of working with leaders, and in my research asking followers what they need during a change in strategy, there are three main ways in which leaders too often send confusing signals to their organizations. Get them right, and you can signal clearly and effectively; fail to pay attention to how and what you are signaling in these three modes, and you will have confusion at best—and at worst, the opposite of the strategic changes you've asked for.

Signal 1: Telling Your Organization About the Outcomes You Want

You'd think this would be the easy bit, but the evidence suggests that this is where leaders most shortchange their organizations. Too many followers tasked with delivering strategic change report that their leaders weren't clear enough about what they wanted the change to achieve or about what it would entail.

It seems the reasons for this are twofold: Leaders too often express what they want in terms not of *outcomes*, but of *tasks*, and they rarely, if ever, make clear the full *extent* of the change they are asking for.

One client I worked with recently—let's call it Sales and Product Co.—was trying to make its business more customer-centric. Its leaders had expressed what they wanted as a list of activities that their middle managers would be asked to work on. There were nine projects. The list gave middle managers clarity about what to do, certainly, but it told them nothing about why they were doing it or how their myriad activities might fit together to create a cohesive program. So we worked with them to reexpress what they wanted as outcome-level targets. "Conduct exit interviews with all departing customers" became "reduce the customer attrition rate," for example. A target to improve cross-selling rates through more outbound calls per month became, simply, "improve profit per customer."

And because the middle managers now knew the target outcomes leaders wanted, within weeks they were able to identify better, smarter, and cheaper ways to deliver them. Instead of nine projects, they settled on just two, which drove alignment across activities as well as accountability for them. And because the two were chosen by people close to the business, who understood the interactions of customer data and processes far better than the senior management team could (or should), the projects had a far better chance of delivering their outcomes. When asked why they knew it was these particular two projects they should work on, the middle managers said, "Well, we knew what the outcomes had to be. And we know how the business works, so it's not that hard." The importance of specifying outcomes for followers, rather than choosing activities for them, was clear.

Why is this signal so hard to get right?

Leadership teams I've worked with have an almost primal urge to give their middle managers a list of activities.

It makes them feel like action is being taken and that they are helping their hard-pressed middle managers by telling them exactly what to do. It's also much easier to jump from "We need to change" to "Here's what to do" than it is to thrash out the difficult trade-offs involved.

Left to their own devices, many leadership teams shortchange the questions of what they want the change to achieve, and why. When we work with leaders, we often have to push them to continue thinking about these questions and to answer them with sufficient clarity. But even as we do, we regularly have someone in the leadership team come up to us in a coffee break and say something along the lines of, "So, all this is great, but when are we going to *get down to it*? You know, talk about what we're actually going to *do*." It usually takes several conversations, and stubbornness, to help them see that this is what they as leaders needed to "get down to"— and, conversely, that until this is done, any scoping out of activities is premature.

In particular, there are four questions that senior teams often don't give enough time to:

1. **Why do we need to change, and why now?** What are the imperatives driving this change? Why is the previous strategy no longer good enough? Where on the P&L are we feeling, or anticipating, pain? Are you sure you want X to change, even if it means you can't have Y anymore?

2. **What is the full extent of the change we need?** Don't underestimate the extent of the change you need, either privately or publicly. However

tempting it is to tell people that this is just an incremental change (when it is nothing of the sort) or however politically expedient it seems to underplay the extent of the change required, a lack of clarity about the extent of the change required will make subsequent conversations about resources and priorities much harder.

3. **If we figure out questions 1 and 2, what should improve as a result, and how will we measure the improvement we've been targeting?** And perhaps most overlooked of all:

4. **How does this new strategy or change link to previous strategies?** Answering this question is critical if leaders are to reduce the confusion that a cumulative overload of strategic or change initiatives—another year, another "strategy"—and their potentially conflicting targets can cause. If leaders can't explain these links clearly, then you need to revisit the need for this change (questions 1–3) or phase out some of the existing initiatives.

Once you have sufficiently clear answers to these four questions, you have the first ingredient for successful signaling.

Signal 2: Personally Living the Change You've Asked For

Living the change you want to see means much more than modeling any behaviors you've asked for; it also means making a myriad of decisions that support the change. It is what David Nadler and Michael Tushman, in their 1990 exploration of how change becomes institutionalized, called "mundane behaviors."[1] It means changing how you spend your time. How you choose to use your most precious, finite resource is a critically important signal you send as a leader. If you're not giving time to the change you've asked for, followers will interpret this change as not really important and will act accordingly. For Sales and Product Co., this meant the C-suite executives routinely scheduling time to discuss progress, and leaving enough space in their calendars to be available to discuss issues and blockages as the need arose.

It also means changing the agenda of senior team meetings and board discussions. For Sales and Product Co., this meant putting "customers" literally at the top of the agenda for every senior team meeting. Before the seemingly tiny change, the C-suite had talked about customer issues after sales, products, and regulation, and just ahead of "any other business." This order had often meant that customer issues didn't get discussed at all or were rushed through by tired execs eager to close the meeting. In an organization that sought to become more customer-focused, this couldn't go on. Talking about customers early in every meeting gave them the priority, and attention, they deserved. It also meant that never again would followers ask their C-suite exec, "What did you discuss at the board meeting?" to hear the answer "We didn't get to the customer stuff."

Why is this signal so hard to get right?

It's partly because carving out time, and making sure you always have spare time in your calendar for strategic issues as they arise, is so much easier than it sounds. You may also have to make this time available for years on end, given how long strategic change takes to embed. That means having to say no to a lot of other people and their priorities, if you are to keep time available for this priority.

And there will be many times when your old, usual issues will feel like such urgent priorities that you will be tempted to get them out of the way first, before turning your attention to the more important strategic stuff. This is a trap. Sort out the most important issue first—and sort it properly. Your business will then be in fundamentally better shape on the urgent issues.

But another reason why personally living the change is a hard signal to send is that sending this signal effectively is a full-time job. Managing yourself—day in and day out, even when you don't feel like it—is hard. One of the leaders I've worked with describes this as "an out-of-body experience," where he is trying to be simultaneously in the moment with someone, listening to them and thinking about the issue, and also *external to himself*, deliberate about how he is showing up and conscious of the impact he is having on those around him. Like all mundane behaviors, it is very easy to not notice that you are not doing them—and that, of course, is precisely when your followers are looking most closely at you.

Signal 3: Resourcing and Measuring the Change You've Asked For

How your organization spends its resources (capital, people, capabilities) and what it chooses to measure are the final critical ways it signals what is important. As a leader, you disproportionately shape these decisions and therefore the clarity of these signals. This means finding the resources needed to deliver the change you've asked for. It doesn't just mean money—though that is important. It also means allocating the right people, with the right level of seniority, experience, and political connections, to work on the change. These are all ways you can signal to the organization that the change is important.

It also means making changes to what you measure, and making these changes early on in the change. All too often, a new change spends its first few quarters being undermeasured because the existing suite of metrics the organization uses haven't been overhauled to reflect the new priorities. If what gets measured is what gets managed, give the change its best chance by signaling as early as possible that new metrics will be introduced to measure, and therefore embed, the change you've asked for.

Why is this signal so hard to send?

Part of the problem is that reallocating resources and changing metrics aren't the glamorous work of strategic change. Rarely are mundane, instrumental, transactional leadership endeavors (such as resourcing or measurement) given much airtime in popular management literature or airport books. The result is that these more mundane aspects of leading change are still regarded as less important by leaders—although they remain some of the most critical signals for followers.

And, of course, making changes to resourcing and metrics takes time. The announcement of the strategic change might have missed the annual planning and budgeting round. While it's painful to face up to, announcing a major change might mean asking people to redo this grunt work. And while those asked to do it may not be immediately enamored with the request, they know the alternative is that they, and everyone else in the organization, will be second-guessing the change until this grunt work is done.

Now, it may take several months to define, agree, baseline, and then measure these new metrics, so start this work early (and just as importantly, talk about the fact that you're doing it). That way you signal to the organization what's coming and that the change is not a passing fad. Send the signal that this change is your priority—and that it will be resourced and measured accordingly.

Your people are looking for signals to help them make sense of what they should do. As a leader, you have disproportionate power to shape these signals—or not. That's especially important when you're asking for change. So supply them with what they need to make sense of it. Be the story you want their children to hear.

Elsbeth Johnson, a former equity analyst and corporate strategist, is a senior lecturer at MIT's Sloan School of Management and the founder of SystemShift, a consulting firm.

NOTE

1. David A. Nadler and Michael L. Tushman, "Beyond the Charismatic Leader: Leadership and Organizational Change," *California Management Review* 32, no. 2 (1990): 77–97.

CHAPTER 14

Strategy Briefing: An Example

by Stephen Bungay

In the decades since Peter Drucker first urged executives to manage by objectives, companies have replaced his famous "letter to the boss" with ever more elaborate and time-consuming processes for setting goals. The result is usually a profusion of measures and targets, finally approved six months into the year they are supposed to cover, that only add to the confusion about what really matters to the business. For most managers, the big unanswered question remains: What do you want *me* to do?

This piece is about how to answer that question. In the following pages you will read about a process I call

---

Adapted from "How to Make the Most of Your Company's Strategy," *Harvard Business Review*, January–February 2011 (product #R1101L).

strategy briefing, a technique derived from the military. Through it, managers and their reports can move together from the uncertainty surrounding seemingly complex goals and performance measures to clarity about just which objectives each person needs to focus on, in what order of priority. The briefing also helps managers set parameters for two variables that are the bedrock of high performance: the extent to which people in an organization act in line with its leaders' intentions, and how much freedom they have to take independent action. In essence, the briefing turns lofty strategic goals into a clear blueprint for execution.

In what follows I'll walk you through the five-step briefing process, illustrating it with a fictional example stitched together from my own experiences as a consultant and a teacher. To conclude I'll explain how to roll the process up, down, and across your organization.

The Road to Confusion Is Paved with Good Intentions

Joe was a star. An engineer, he also had an MBA and worked at a large, well-established information services company. A year after moving into product development, he was asked to set up a low-cost R&D center in Asia. By introducing new, less expensive offerings, the company hoped to fend off increasing competition from cheaper rivals.

Six months into the project, Joe convened an off-site. After presenting the company's goals and challenges, he asked the people attending for thoughts on how they could help meet them. After a few moments' silence, one of the senior technicians raised her hand. "I don't want to sound negative," she said, "but what exactly are we really trying to achieve?"

Joe was taken aback. "It's perfectly clear, isn't it? We're creating a new center to develop low-cost products. We've got two years. You know the situation, and you know the company's strategy. I just went through it."

"Sure," came the reply, "but frankly, I'm still confused. There's lots of stuff in our goals about shareholder value, reinventing ourselves, thinking globally, and embracing change. There's stuff about being innovative and delivering superior customer satisfaction, and there are targets for increasing revenue, lowering costs, and raising margins. Well, I don't get it. From where I sit, the sky's falling in. We're in a deep recession, the competition is eating our lunch, revenues are falling, margins are shot to bits, customers are starting to hate us, and all anyone seems to care about is getting rid of people to save money. Some of us are probably next. Where are we in all this? What are we supposed to do?"

Joe sensed that he needed to take control. "OK," he said, "I hear you. And you're right. Let's sit down and work it out now so we're all singing from the same sheet. Let's not just talk; let's write it down, so we all know exactly what we are about."

Step 1: State Your Intent

Joe went over to a flip chart and wrote down "Task + Purpose." Under "Task" he wrote "what," and under "Purpose" he wrote "why." As he turned back to his audience, he saw to his surprise that people had perked up.

"So we'll answer those questions, right?" he said. "Here and now."

The discussion began as usual with an aspiration. It was not long before the words *world class* were uttered, as someone suggested that the team's purpose was to "build a world-class development facility." Some of the team members liked that. Others rolled their eyes. "Look," somebody piped up, "that's an aspiration anyone could have. It makes no difference; it's vague and has nothing to do with our situation." The first version was crossed out. The purpose became "to build a new development facility."

"But that's just a description of what we're doing," came the objection. "Isn't the question, What are we trying to achieve?"

"We need to reduce costs," came the answer. So perhaps that was the "why."

Joe called a halt to the increasingly fractious discussion. "Let's step back a second," he suggested. "What is the situation?" He tried to sum it up, for both himself and the others:

"The company's revenues are declining by 10% a year, in part because we're in the worst market in history but also because we're losing share. Our cost base is 30% too high, our products are old, and customer satisfaction is falling. We claim to be innovative, but new-product development is blocked. Our job, surely, is to unblock it. If we do that, it will reduce operating costs and improve customer satisfaction, and that will help sales."

Joe felt somewhat liberated by what he had just said. Like everyone else, he had a mental list of what needed to be done. The company always had to improve costs, revenues, margins, and service. But he had just articulated the relationship between them for the first time. New-product development was the link that completed the chain. He realized that for him success meant getting products out now.

The discussion continued. Half an hour later, the group had its first answer on the flip chart:

What: *To significantly reduce time to market for development, enhancements, and support of high-quality products to our customers in a cost-effective manner.*

Why: *To help aggressively grow our revenues and increase our margins.*

During lunch Joe went outside to think. He did not like what the team had written. It was too broad and too unrealistic. How was the firm going to aggressively grow in the current market? He ruefully realized that he should have thought about this long ago. He needed to set the scene for his people.

Step 2: Try Again—This Time in Context

Joe went back to the flip chart and turned down a new sheet. At the top of it he wrote, "Context." Then he listed four observations:

1. The company's market share is being eroded by competitors under some of the most difficult trading conditions in our history.

2. The loss of share must be halted, or we will have no basis for future growth.

3. Customer service is the key to halting this decline, but with the existing product line, it's impossible to deliver outstanding service at acceptable margins.

4. With the current loss of accounts, every day that passes makes recovery more difficult.

The group came back in as he finished. "Does that help?" he asked. There were nods as people read what he had written. "Actually, we've got a crucial role in all of this, haven't we?" observed one of the head programmers.

"And," somebody added, "if it's true, it means that what matters is time. We've got to speed things up."

"Is that right?" someone else asked. "Is that what the company wants us to do?"

"Let's look again at what the company strategy document says," Joe replied. He fiddled around on his laptop until the words of the corporation filled the screen:

We are committed to delivering Great Service to our customers. This will require us to build a strong service-based culture. This will be achieved by a combination of improved customer and market segmentation capability, improved customer service processes and tools, and, significantly, specific customer-focused behaviors' being constantly demonstrated both internally and with external customers. The goal is to reshape the business to deliver superior shareholder value over a sustained period.

The group stared blankly at the screen. "Marketing wrote that," someone commented.

"More like HR," said another person. "Though finance finally got their oar in at the end."

"Think about what's behind it," Joe said. "It says there is going to be a change. The clock's ticking. We have to give customers better service than our competitors do if we are to get them back, and we've got to make money as well."

"So how do we fit in?" someone asked.

"If the company is to compete on service, it needs us to come up with the products to enable it to do so," Joe replied. "It used to be all about technology and features, but it's a service game now. I was talking to the head of technology about it. She wants a coherent suite of products, not the mess we've got now, with different offerings for every region and every client. I've talked to the head of Asia as well. The costs are killing us. We have to make some hard choices. Sales won't like it, but there it is. It is our call. Why don't we try to write it down, simply, and work out what it is that senior management wants us to do? What was their intention when they wrote all this?"

Forty minutes and several flip-chart sheets later, Joe's group had a formulation, which it decided to call "Higher Intent." The formulation read:

Two Levels Up (Corporate)

What: *To transform the company within the next three years.*

Why: *To deliver superior service and financial performance.*

One Level Up (Technology Group)

What: *To develop and support a coherent product line that is easy to service.*

Why: *To allow sales and marketing to grow revenues.*

"Our job," said Joe, "is to fulfill the technology group's intent in Asia. Their intent tells us a few things that should drive every decision. The new products have to be simpler to service, or they're no good. They have to fit in with what's being done globally, and the local salespeople will have to live with that—no more customization. We've got to design products with sales and marketing to make sure they'll sell. They have to be low cost or we can't make money. And we've got to move fast. Now let's look at our earlier intent statement again. What do *we* have to do *now*?"

The immediate needs were defensive. There was no way anyone could grow revenues and margins in the current climate. The firm had to stop the erosion of market share. It was also clear that the company had to get something new out the door that year. Moreover, Joe's group needed to focus its efforts; more than 250 products, in all stages, were in the pipeline, and the group would have to decide which ones would make the most difference.

Finally, the team came up with this statement of intent:

What: *To accelerate delivery of critical products to market.*

Why: *To enable sales channels to halt market share erosion by year-end.*

"Is this ambitious enough?" someone asked. "It doesn't sound particularly inspiring."

"This is enough," said Joe. "If we give ourselves a target we can't achieve, we're setting ourselves up for failure. But that reminds me, we need some measures so that we know what we're doing is working. We haven't finished yet."

Step 3: Set Your Measures

Joe and his team determined that to achieve the objectives they had just outlined, they needed to focus on three things—time, market share, and costs. They expressed each in terms of a goal:

1. Deliver agreed product set by year-end and on budget.

2. See that total market share in Asia at the end of the year equals the share at the beginning of the year.

3. Reduce operating costs for development in the region by 20%.

There was a pause. They were all studying the flip chart. Someone frowned. "We ourselves cannot stop market share from declining," he said. "Do we want to be measured on that?"

"Strictly speaking, no," replied Joe, "but it is the purpose behind everything we are doing. If the rate at which we're losing share goes down, we'll know what we're doing is working, even if we don't hit the target. If we don't look at it, we might be barking up the wrong tree."

"What about what we *are* measured on?" someone piped up. "We've all got targets. Dozens of them." So they had, including Joe himself. Part of his bonus was tied to the number of new products delivered. Optimizing that would not be difficult—he could just go for the easy development projects nearest completion. But they might not have the most impact.

"Look," he said, "I'll make a commitment to you. I will renegotiate the targets for this group. I'll explain what we are doing and that the measures are just there to tell us whether we're successful or not. The outcome is what we're trying to optimize. The measures are the dashboard. We should not confuse the readings on it with what we really want to do, which is to arrive on time at our destination. When we've worked out who is doing what, I'll measure your performance on how well you accomplish your assigned tasks. What I want to know from you now is what you think those tasks should be."

Step 4: Define the Tasks Implied by Your Intent

The people in Joe's group started by looking at what they were actually doing. They were involved in three types of activity: growing an offshore facility, improving costs and efficiency, and working on various initiatives related to morale and customer service. They decided to do only what was essential and to sideline initiatives not related to their intent.

Then they realized they'd left something out. Someone needed to figure out which products were critical to the company's goals—an issue no one was addressing. That was the first task. The team members knew that some work on costs would have to continue but that it was even more important to speed up development and deliver something good to the sales force. To ensure that people didn't get distracted from that task, they decided to dedicate half the staff solely to development and have the rest work only on enhancements and support. In sum, four main tasks were implied by the intent:

1. Identify the critical products.

2. Accelerate development of those products.

3. Create enhancements to existing products faster and provide more-responsive product support.

4. Reduce costs.

If Joe and his group accomplished all those goals, they would achieve their intent—and be heroes. But suppose they had to make trade-offs? Joe looked at the list. "In all of this," he asked, "what's really vital? If we had to cut, where would we cut last?"

The team members had a debate. Though they needed to define the critical products, they could get that broadly right. They had to reduce costs, but if they failed, they could accept low margins for a time. The thing that mattered most was the fast development of new products—if they didn't get that right this year, all else would be in vain. Joe went back to the chart and drew a red circle around "Accelerate development." Next to it, he wrote, "Main effort."

It was time for a break. Joe went for a stroll outside and reflected. The group had started with a list of things to do that were only loosely related and varied in importance. Putting that to one side, the participants had thought through what needed to be done most so that the tasks were prioritized. They had filled in a key missing piece in their to-do list—identifying the critical products. And they also had a list of tasks that didn't overlap, so people could tackle them without getting in one another's way. Now Joe wanted to assign the tasks to his people and have them come up with a plan for accomplishing them. He didn't want to dictate how to do things; his reports all knew their jobs better than he did and needed to put some creative thought into their plans. He wanted to give them space. But how could he set the right parameters for them?

Joe went back in, and as the team reassembled, he wrote a new heading on each of two flip charts: "Freedoms" and "Constraints." The brainstorming began. A quarter of an hour later, the list under "Freedoms" included "senior management support," "motivated employees," and "the importance of new products." A longer list under "Constraints" included "concerns about our ability to deliver," "customer reluctance to adopt new products," "competitor activity," and "organizational complexity."

Step 5: Define the Boundaries

Joe stepped back. Everyone looked a bit blank. The lists weren't very helpful. They looked like a list of good things and a list of bad things. The bad ones were more complaints than constraints, plus a few worries. The lists didn't show what people were or were not free to do.

"Let's try again," he said. "Let's really try to think about what we can or can't do. Let's begin with the constraints."

It soon became clear that there were two big ones: They were trying to optimize time, but cost and quality imposed boundaries. Within a few minutes there was an earnest debate among the participants, which started to get passionate and technical at the same time. Joe stopped it. "We've just identified another aspect of the tasks," he said. "We're going to have to work this out as we go. Let's not assume we know the answer already." He wrote down the two constraints:

1. Product quality—to be defined with reference to customer needs and the service organization.

2. Product cost—requirements set by budget and competitive benchmarks.

Though Joe's group had no control over those constraints, it had to find out what they were. He and his team realized that by defining their boundaries, they were also identifying whom they had to talk to both inside and outside the organization. The discussion became more concrete and more focused. They identified two more constraints and a question:

3. The requirement to reduce the number of development centers—to be agreed on with the head of Asia.

4. Product obsolescence program—to be agreed on with global product management.

5. Who has final decision on new-product development projects?

As he looked at these, Joe realized that he had defined his own role. His job as leader was to manage the team's boundaries. Tackling the first four constraints would involve working with the decision makers and ensuring that the team's proposals were good enough to be accepted. The fifth item on the list was something he had to clarify. He made a note to himself to raise the issues with both his regional boss and his functional boss when he saw them next.

The shadows were lengthening and people were tired; time to call it a day. "Well," said Joe, after he'd assigned the four tasks to different managers, "I want each of you leading a task to come back to me by the end of next week to tell me how you are going to tackle it. Now, let's have a drink before we head to the airport."

The Rollout

A single strategy briefing like the one I've just described can help an individual team perform better, but the real magic happens when briefings are held throughout an organization. When, at the end of the story, Joe assigns the tasks and asks his reports to develop their own plans, it means that they must now conduct their own briefings with their subordinates.

In each of his subordinates' statements of intent the "why" will be Joe's "what"—to accelerate delivery to market of critical products—and the "what" will be the task Joe assigned that person. So for the first of his direct reports, the intent will be "to identify the critical set of products in order to accelerate their delivery to market"; for the second, "to speed up development in order to accelerate the delivery of critical products to market"; and so on. Each of those four people's direct reports will then work out their implied tasks and pass those along to their subordinates with their "whats." The process will continue until no further analysis is necessary. In this way a company's strategy is translated into a set of discrete but linked elements that give a clear view downward toward actions and upward toward the company's strategy, and align functions across the organization.

The rollout must also incorporate a feedback process in which the leader of a group that has just conducted a briefing presents the output to the people they report to. In Joe's case, this "back-briefing" should involve a discussion of the metrics that he and his group came up with, which differed from the official targets.

In back-briefings three things happen. First, the unit doing the back-briefing checks its understanding of the direction it has received or worked out. Second, higher-ups gain clarity about the implications of the direction they originally gave and may revise it as a result—as Joe's bosses would probably do for the metrics. Third, it provides an opportunity to ensure alignment across the organization as well as up and down; if Joe's reports give their back-briefings to him together, he can check for gaps, overlaps, and coherence.

Effective briefing helps unlock hidden sources of productivity. It offers a practical way to ensure that the people in your company are both strategically aligned and operationally autonomous, a combination that has been the hallmark of high-performance organizations for 2,000 years—since the days of the Roman army. Now part of military practice throughout NATO, the strategy briefing technique has a 150-year track record, going back to the 19th-century Prussian army, of enabling forces to cope with the fast-changing uncertainties of warfare. Given that the business environment has become equally unpredictable, it's time for companies to adopt it as well. It may be the best investment in time you will ever make.

Stephen Bungay is the author of *The Art of Action: How Leaders Close the Gaps Between Plans, Actions and Results*. He works as an independent speaker and consultant, based in London.

Manage Strategic Initiatives

CHAPTER 15

How to Prioritize Your Company's Strategic Projects

by Antonio Nieto-Rodriguez

Every organization needs what I call a "hierarchy of purpose." Without one, it is almost impossible to prioritize effectively.

When I first joined BNP Paribas Fortis, for example, two younger and more dynamic banks had just overtaken us. Although we had been a market leader for many years, our new products had been launched several months later than the competition—in fact, our time to market had doubled over the previous three years.

Adapted from "How to Prioritize Your Company's Projects," on hbr.org, December 13, 2016 (product #H03BU7).

Behind that problem was a deeper one: We had more than 100 large projects (each worth over €500,000) underway. No one had a clear view of the status of those investments, or even the anticipated benefits. The bank was using a project management tool, but the lack of discipline in keeping it up to date made it largely fruitless. Capacity, not strategy, was determining which projects launched and when. If people were available, the project was launched. If not, it stalled or was killed.

Prioritization at a strategic and operational level is often the difference between success and failure. But many organizations do it badly.

Take another example: a postal service company delivering packages to customers. Like many other postal services, the company has been struggling to survive in an era of increasing competition and digital substitutes. Senior leaders gathered employees together at a series of town hall events where the CEO asked them to focus on two operational priorities: efficiency (reducing delivery times) and customer satisfaction (ensuring customers had a good experience).

One employee, Mary, got the message. And it worked fine until she was out delivering packages and was met at the door by an elderly man who asked her to come in and talk for a while. Mary's natural inclination was to spend a little time with the lonely old man. It would be a kind thing to do, and surely it would also increase customer satisfaction. But then she froze. What about efficiency? If she spent even a few minutes chatting with her customer, her delivery times would suffer. What was she meant to do? Thousands of employees at this company were facing similar trade-offs every day.

The predicament is a typical one. The senior management of the postal company thought they had communicated clear priorities, but in fact they had created an operational dilemma that resulted from strategic confusion.

Contrast this with other successful companies. The European budget airline Ryanair, for example, is absolutely clear that it is a no-frills operation where efficiency is the operational priority—it takes precedence over customer service. The people who work for Ryanair know what the priority is and thus know how to allocate their time on the job.

Prioritizing increases the success rates of strategic projects, increases the alignment and focus of senior management teams around strategic goals, clears all doubts for the operational teams when faced with decisions, and most important, builds an execution mindset and culture.

Of course, sometimes leaders simply make the wrong decisions; they prioritize the wrong thing. But in my 20 years as an executive, the problem I see more often is that leaders don't make decisions at all. They don't clearly signal their intent about what matters.

Among the organizations I have worked with—and others, such as Apple, Amazon, Lego, Ikea, and Western Union, that have highly developed senses of priorities— the payoffs are considerable. Companies that start prioritizing can experience significant reductions in costs (in my experience, roughly 15%) as less-vital activities are cut and duplicated efforts are consolidated.

The number of priorities an organization admits to is revealing. It is notable that if the risk appetite of a senior executive team is very low (or if they are not able or inclined to make the tough choices), they will tend to have a generous portfolio of priorities; they don't want to take the risk of not being compliant, missing a market opportunity, not having the latest technologies, and so on. But from what I've seen, the most successful executives tend to be more risk-taking and have a laser-like focus on a small number of priorities. These executives know what matters today and tomorrow. At the extreme, this might mean simply having a single priority. The more focus, the better.

The Hierarchy of Purpose

I have over 20 years of experience in prioritizing, selecting, and managing projects. In that time, I have developed a simple framework that I call the "hierarchy of purpose." It is a tool that executive teams can use to help them prioritize strategic initiatives and projects:

- **Purpose.** What is the purpose of the organization, and how is that purpose best pursued? What is the strategic vision supporting this purpose?

- **Priorities.** Given the stated purpose and vision, what matters most to the organization now and in the future? What are its priorities now and over the next two to five years?

- **Projects.** Based on the answers to the first two points, which projects or initiatives are the most strategic and should be resourced to the hilt? Which projects align with the purpose, vision, and priorities, and which should be stopped or scrapped?

- **People.** Now that there is clarity around the strategic priorities and the projects that matter most, who are the best people to execute on those projects?

- **Performance.** Traditionally, project performance indicators are tied to inputs (for example, scope, cost, and time). They are much easier to track than outputs (such as benefits, impact, and goals). However, despite the difficulty companies have in tracking outputs, the outputs are what really matter. What are the precise outcome-related targets that will measure real performance and value creation? Reduce your attention to inputs and focus on those instead.

At best, prioritizing enhances the strategic dialogue and the alignment at the top of the organization, from where it is then cascaded to the rest of the organization. Once you lead the executive team to understand this, priorities become embedded in the organization and its corporate culture.

Think of your organization's priorities. Are all of your diverse activities prioritized in the best interests of the organization as a whole? What is the best use of the organization's existing and future financial and operational capacities? How would your priorities change in case of a sudden economic downturn?

A well-communicated sense of organizational priorities helps to align most of the projects and programs in an organization to its strategies. But the reality of an organization is much more complex than many suggest. Sometimes the strategic objectives are not clear or are nonexistent. Often there is a gap and lack of alignment between the corporate strategic objectives and the ones from the different business units, departments, or functions.

In reality, it is impossible to match all of an organization's projects and programs to strategic objectives. Ensuring that at least the most important projects and programs—let's say the top 20—are fully aligned with the strategic objectives is more achievable.

By applying the hierarchy of purpose, executives learn that changing priorities is a fact of organizational life. Indeed, every time an organization stops a priority, the organization becomes more focused. Every terminated priority is an opportunity to learn and do better next time. Priorities change and, if managed successfully, have the capacity to fundamentally change organizations, but only if top management makes tough choices.

———————

Antonio Nieto-Rodriguez is the author of the *Harvard Business Review Project Management Handbook* (Harvard Business Review Press, 2019), the HBR article "The

Project Economy Has Arrived," and five other books. He is a pioneer and authority in advising senior leaders on delivering strategic projects and teaching modern project management to more than 100 corporations. Antonio is a visiting professor in seven top business schools. His research and work have elevated project management to be a C-suite topic, an achievement recognized by Thinkers50. Fellow and former chair of the Project Management Institute, where he launched the Brightline Initiative, he is the founder of Projects & Co and the Strategy Implementation Institute. Contact him through his website, antonionietorodriguez.com.

CHAPTER 16

Six Questions to Ask Before You Begin a Big Project

by Antonio Nieto-Rodriguez and Whitney Johnson

Knowing when to *start* a project is a key factor to its success. And yet it's a strategic talent very few companies have developed. If you begin a project too soon, chances are high that it will miss its deadline—*if* it doesn't fail outright.

A great example of this is Google Glass, which was launched on April 15, 2013. Google Glass had made very little progress two years after its release and, as a result,

---

Adapted from "6 Questions to Ask Before Starting a Big Project," on hbr.org, February 12, 2020 (product #H05F6J).

was discontinued in 2015. This led to confusion about whether it was an actual finished product or just a prototype. And despite bold attempts to market the product (skydivers, fashion shows, etc.), it never really brought anything truly practical or revolutionary to the table.

Apple's iPhone is a counterexample. Creating the iPhone was first suggested to Steve Jobs in 2001. He loved the idea, especially the possibility of disrupting the telecom sector, one of the most profitable and fastest-growing industries at that time. But despite the attractive vision, he refused to launch a project to realize it.

Jobs made it clear to his executive team that the focus, energy, and key resources of Apple had to be devoted to its two strategic priorities: growing iTunes and consolidating the iPod as the new gadget for listening to music. He assigned a few engineers to further explore the smartphone concept, build some prototypes, and partner with other telecom players. Not until 2004, three years after the initial proposal, was an official project established. Amazing, right?

As we can see in these two examples, deciding when to invest your company's scarce resources in a project is of strategic importance. Yet, there is currently no management framework available to help executives or individuals with the vital decision of when the *right time* has arrived.

Applying the S-Curve Model to Project Development

The S-curve framework was originally popularized by communication theorist and sociologist E. M. Rogers to gauge how rapidly new innovations would penetrate the market, be adopted, and become widely diffused. The S-curve can also help decision makers envision when it's the right time to initiate a project and thereafter model its progress.

The base of the S-curve is a phase of slow, low growth. Slow is a relative term; in our environment of rapid innovation and change, no one can afford to be too slow. But for an enterprise that is exploring an idea, and the possibility of a project to bring that idea to fruition, the base of the curve represents a period of investigation when relatively few resources have been committed. The purpose of this phase is to ascertain whether there is really an opportunity in an idea—or not. During this phase is when you should seek answers to six important, foundational questions.

Has the project been done before?

It's important to determine, to the degree possible, if there is a market for a proposed product or service. To do this, explore what problem it will solve for target customers, and whether the need for a solution exists, or whether you will be going head-to-head against already established competitors. If so, is there a distinguishing feature to your idea that can give it a competitive edge? Define the unique niche you anticipate filling in the marketplace. The newer the idea, the more time required at the low end of the S-curve to explore it—avoid starting the project right away.

Is the project part of your core business and will it leverage your strengths? Or will you be venturing into something completely new?

The further from the core business, the more time you will need to spend at the lower end of the S-curve. Also, consider the number of projects you already have outside your core business. Too many will jeopardize the project to the point of putting your company at risk. A good distribution of projects used by some leading organizations is 60% in the core business, 30% in the adjacent business area, and 10% far from the core.

Can you clearly define the scope? Do you know what the project will produce and look like when completed?

How many of the ultimate requirements do you know (1% to 100%)? If you have less than 50% clarity of what the project will deliver, keep exploring and iterating to better define the project. Traditional project management theory teaches us to have 100% of the requirements defined at the beginning of the project, but we know this is hardly the case. Aim at having 80% to 90% of the requirements defined before moving to the full-blown project stage.

What is the investment cost?

This can include determining what resources will be required—financial, human, expertise, management time—and determining whether they are available in-house or will have to be sourced externally. Is this something we can and want to commit to? Remember that projects are costly and have a high probability of costing more than originally planned. This is not only financial—they often take up more resources and management time as well. Therefore, it is important to clarify before starting the project who is going to pay for it, as well as ensuring the commitment of the resources, including time dedicated by executives. These are all important decisions to be considered at the lower end of the S-curve.

Do you have buy-in from key leaders and the wider organization?

Excellent ideas and brilliant projects have become monumental failures due to lack of buy-in from key stakeholders. The exploration phase should coalesce critical mass around the project, enhancing its viability. Are you getting buy-in from crucial stakeholders? Is there movement or inertia around the idea within the organization? If the institutional will is there, the other necessary resources are likely to be in the pipeline. (For more on how to ensure leadership buy-in and support, see the sidebar "How to Work with an Executive Sponsor.")

What is the time line?

Projects that languish when they should be charging ahead are costly and unlikely to produce satisfactory results. Establish a time line and a schedule for the achievement of necessary benchmarks. Tight milestones

HOW TO WORK WITH AN EXECUTIVE SPONSOR

by Ron Ashkenas

Over the past decade, the role of the "executive sponsor" has become well accepted and even ubiquitous in organizations. The sponsor makes sure that the project's goals are aligned with overall company strategy, garners support (and overcomes resistance) from other senior executives, and provides ongoing direction as the effort unfolds. In contrast with the project leader, who focuses mostly on day-to-day execution, the sponsor role is much more strategic, focusing on creating conditions for success instead of tactical implementation.

But how do you work effectively with an executive sponsor? Let me suggest two steps.

First, before launching a new project, the sponsor and the project leader should meet to set, clarify, and align expectations.

This is particularly important if the sponsor was not actively involved in the project conception (and was only asked to be the sponsor after the fact) and may not understand the background and issues. The project leader can address the amount of guidance, senior-level support, and resources that would be needed for the project. The sponsor can analyze and sharpen the project's objectives, establish key milestones, and approve a review and communication schedule. For this to work, however, both have to be able to talk candidly, which requires courage on the part of the project leader and encouragement on the part of the sponsor.

Next, the sponsor and the project leader must be realistic about how much time and effort will be required from the executive level.
If the sponsor wants to take project sponsorship seriously, she should be clear about the commitment. She also has to accept accountability for seeing these through. Setting up key meetings, reviews, and checkpoints can cut down on time, but it takes a strong emotional commitment to do what is necessary to help see the project through. This can be incredibly rewarding, too, since it provides an opportunity to work with senior colleagues and be viewed as an enterprise leader.

Having an executive-level sponsor can be crucial for shepherding major projects, particularly those that cut across functions. But for this to happen, both the executive and the project leader must be clear about their mutual expectations and time commitments for ensuring a success.

———

Ron Ashkenas is a coauthor of the *Harvard Business Review Leader's Handbook* and a partner emeritus at Schaffer Consulting. His previous books include *The Boundaryless Organization*, *The GE Work-Out*, and *Simply Effective*.

Adapted from "How to Be an Effective Executive Sponsor," on hbr.org, May 18, 2015 (product #H022VP).

focus organizations and teams, so use them wisely. Be doubtful about time lines of projects that don't spend time in the exploration phase.

Eventually there is an inflection point when it's time to pull the plug on the idea or actively develop it. This knee of the S-curve is the place to officially create a project, if you're going to forge ahead. Resources should have been assembled, personnel emplaced, objectives articulated, and a time frame established. The project begins after critical needs have been identified and addressed, not before. The steep back of the S-curve models a period of explosive growth. When a project launches, it should be ready to *go*, rapidly ascending this part of the curve.

We all want to create well-grounded projects that have a higher likelihood of success. The low end of the S-curve exploration is the opportunity to determine the viability of an idea and assemble the puzzle pieces required to carry it out, *or* to determine that it's an idea whose time has not come—and maybe never will. The best time to terminate a project is before it's been initiated. Starting a project only when ready to execute as expeditiously and efficiently as possible maximizes the opportunity for success and the return on the resources invested in it.

———————

Antonio Nieto-Rodriguez is the author of the *Harvard Business Review Project Management Handbook* (Harvard Business Review Press, 2019), the HBR article "The Project Economy Has Arrived," and five other books. He is a pioneer and authority in advising senior leaders on delivering strategic projects and teaching modern project management to more than 100 corporations. Antonio is a visiting professor in seven top business schools. His research and work have elevated project management to be a C-suite topic, an achievement recognized by Thinkers50. Fellow and former chair of the Project Management Institute, where he launched the Brightline Initiative, he is the founder of Projects & Co and the Strategy Implementation Institute. Contact Antonio through his website, antonionietorodriguez.com. **Whitney Johnson** is the CEO of Disruption Advisors, a tech-enabled talent-development company, and the author of *Smart Growth: How to Grow Your People to Grow Your Company* (Harvard Business Review Press, 2022).

CHAPTER 17

Start Stopping Faster

by Darrell Rigby, Sarah Elk, and Steve Berez

Business executives could learn a lot from cheetahs, Earth's most agile land animals. Though their ancestors ran only about 20 miles per hour, today's cats can accelerate from zero to 60 within three seconds—faster than a Corvette Twin Turbo or a Ferrari Enzo. But speed alone is not what makes cheetahs such awesome hunters. Computer models show that the best predictor of a successful hunt is not a cheetah's top speed; rather, it's how fast it stops and turns.[1]

There is an important parallel to the executive hunt for innovations. Whether they are developing new

Adapted from content posted on hbr.org, September 22, 2020 (product #H05VKS).

products or processes, or overhauling old ways of doing business, it's not enough that organizations pursue new ideas faster. Unless they develop new muscles for skillfully decelerating and adapting to unexpected twists and turns, they are likely to come up empty-handed. It's one of the most common laments of executives struggling to increase their organization's adaptability: "We are terrible at stopping work, even when it's obvious that the work is a complete waste of time and money." This is as true for existing business lines and processes that live on budget season after budget season zombie-like as it is for a once-bright new idea that simply isn't panning out.

The cost of this problem is higher than managers imagine. Gary Hamel and Michele Zanini, coauthors of the book *Humanocracy*, estimate that as of 2020 the cost of bureaucratic waste had hit $10 trillion and was growing.[2] Between 70% and 90% of innovations fail, and healthy operations grow weaker every day that they must subsidize foundering projects kept alive by political inertia rather than potential payoff.[3] When power is determined by the amount of resources controlled, as it so often is in business, admitting failure and surrendering resources is rare.

Since stopping things is so very hard, executives make starting them even harder, dampening innovation. They raise investment hurdle rates, demand more detailed analyses, and add layers of scrutiny. Sadly, these actions don't improve decisions so much as damage speed to market and competitive positioning. Failures mount. Eventually, the horde of failing projects grows too large to ignore. Managers cull some large percentage of their people, traumatize the organization, and launch the doom loop all over again.

There is another way. Organizations *can* evolve, and by focusing on three specific things, they can improve their own agility and start stopping things faster.

Make More Decisions Reversible

While researching our book *Doing Agile Right*, we learned from former Amazon executive Jason Goldberger that in order to accelerate innovation, founder Jeff Bezos purposefully encourages executives to make decisions reversible, which ensures that a company won't have to live with bad consequences for very long. It thwarts risk aversion and accelerates experimentation.

"If you tell people to innovate without making mistakes, you will kill innovation," Goldberger explains. "But if you tell people to innovate and not worry about mistakes that are quickly reversible, you free them to test and learn in more agile ways."

Unfortunately, not many companies run this way. Far too many investment proposals plan for premature and irreversible scaling. They call for large up-front investments and predict delayed, hockey-stick-shaped revenues and profits. When revenue and profit fail to materialize, it seems too late to stop. The payoff must be just around the corner. "Why, we would be crazy to stop now," executives tell themselves. And so, throwing good money after bad drags on.

One way to break this habit is to run the business the way a savvy venture capitalist invests. Recognize business plans for what they really are: business experiments.

Break large, risky gambles into a series of smaller, smarter tests. Clarify the hypotheses, the best ways to test them, and the metrics that will signal whether to persist, pivot, or pause. Avoid premature scaling—hiring too many people, building too much capacity, doing too much marketing—before key assumptions have been validated. Match costs to revenues. Start by confining experiments to affordable, adaptable, and reversible microcosms of the ultimate solution by limiting geographies, customer segments, or product lines.

Look at DoorDash, the door-to-door delivery company. DoorDash has ridden a surge in demand due to the Covid-19 pandemic, but back in 2013, when it began raising what would eventually become a total of $2.5 billion, venture capitalists didn't just back up a Brink's truck of money to the startup. The risks were too high, and such a move would have limited investors' ability to spur strategic change when necessary. Instead, venture capitalists phased in their investment over 11 rounds of funding.

In the 2016 round, when questions about the viability of its strategy reportedly led to its shares selling at a lower price than earlier rounds, the company made important changes. DoorDash added new services for restaurants and adjusted pay for drivers. Market share increased, as have subsequent valuations.

DoorDash is still not profitable, and its ultimate success is far from guaranteed. But its venture backers have clear and frequent opportunities to change how they invest and influence company direction. Investors can decelerate, pivot, and stop.

Some corporations are already applying this model. Executives review new projects and existing business lines quarterly, utilize fast feedback loops, create rough prototypes, and rely on objective metrics to test key hypotheses. All this makes it possible to more dynamically adjust plans and allocate resources.

Make Work More Visible

It's hard to improve or stop unproductive work if you can't see what work is being done and how well it's going. Too many companies are flying blind.

Executives can inspect physical facilities and assess whether to refurbish or bulldoze them. They can see inventories piling up and decide whether to finish them or write them off. The intangible work of most technology, marketing, and other departments, however, is often invisible to leadership teams.

Increasing visibility is good for everyone. It helps senior executives uncover valuable initiatives, recognize the people pushing them, and accelerate their progress. It allows employees to see projects related to their own jobs, learn from them, and identify where their expertise could solve perplexing problems or save time and money. It makes it easier for everyone to identify duplicative work and triggers discussions about whether overlapping teams should collaborate or compete. It helps teams working on interdependent steps coordinate and minimize delays.

Imagine a system that enables authorized employees to see all work streams, who is on each team, what else they are working on, and how the work is progressing.

Imagine tagging the work of each team with descriptors such as strategic priority, targeted customers, expected economic value, and progress against plans. Perhaps employees could even express how confident they are in each team's success. These systems actually exist—project and portfolio management software, objectives and key results trackers, talent management systems, and workforce analytics—and they are getting better.

Overpower Fear

They say the first rule of daredevil airplane wing-walking is, "Don't let go of what you've got until you get hold of something better." Astute leaders realize that fearful workers will cling to the current work no matter how unproductive. They do several things to overcome that fear. One we've already discussed: They reduce the cost of stopping projects (for example, by conducting experiments).

Another way is to reward people who learn valuable lessons by taking prudent risks, even if the immediate outcome was disappointing. In some cases, this may mean keeping the bold objective but adapting the approach as conditions or capabilities change. When Bezos wanted to enable third-party sellers to sell new or used products on Amazon, the company initially failed: The 1999 launches of Amazon Auctions and zShops both fizzled. But Amazon Marketplace, launched soon after, was a success. It now accounts for more than half of all units sold by the company.

Finally, giving people more opportunities if their current project fails reduces the likelihood that they'll stick with a bad idea longer than they should. Successful companies build a strong and visible backlog of compelling opportunities. They make it clear that until existing projects that aren't panning out have stopped, new initiatives can't be launched. And they redeploy people from the former to the latter as a matter of policy and offer training to ease the transition. In time, the fear of missing out on something better starts to overpower the fear of loss.

In a world of increasingly unpredictable change—where opportunities are constantly zigging and zagging like spry gazelles—running at higher speeds is not enough. Businesses must evolve to match their acceleration muscle with faster stopping and turning skills. As they do, their hunt for growth will grow more fruitful, their competitive capabilities will strengthen, and their position in the food chain will climb.

Darrell Rigby is a partner in the Boston office of Bain & Company. He heads the firm's global agile enterprise practice. He is the author of *Winning in Turbulence* (Harvard Business Review Press, 2009). **Sarah Elk** is a partner in Bain & Company's Chicago office and heads its global people and organization practice. **Steve Berez** is a partner in Bain & Company's Boston office and a founder of its enterprise technology practice. They are the coauthors of *Doing Agile Right: Transformation Without Chaos* (Harvard Business Review Press, 2020).

NOTES

1. Elizabeth Pennisi, "Cheetah Agility More Important Than Speed," *Science*, June 12, 2013, https://www.science.org/content/article/cheetah-agility-more-important-speed.

2. Doug Kirkpatrick, "Taking the Sword to Bureaucracy," *Forbes*, September 3, 2020, https://www.forbes.com/sites/forbesspeakers/2020/09/03/taking-the-sword-to-bureaucracy/?sh=5226735e7dcb.

3. Darrell K. Rigby et al., "Agile Innovation," Bain & Company, April 19, 2016, https://www.bain.com/insights/agile-innovation/.

Track Performance and Ensure Collaboration

CHAPTER 18

Don't Let Metrics Undermine Your Business

by Michael Harris and Bill Tayler

Tying performance metrics to strategy has become an accepted best practice over the past few decades. Strategy is abstract by definition, but metrics give strategy form, allowing our minds to grasp it more readily. With metrics, Ford Motor Company's onetime strategy "Quality is job one" could be translated into Six Sigma performance standards. Apple's "Think different" and Samsung's "Create the future" could be linked to the amount of sales from new products. If strategy is the blueprint

---

Adapted from an article in *Harvard Business Review*, September–October 2019 (product #R1905C).

for building an organization, metrics are the concrete, wood, drywall, and bricks.

But there's a hidden trap in this organizational architecture: A company can easily lose sight of its strategy and instead focus strictly on the metrics that are meant to *represent* it. For an extreme example of this problem, look to Wells Fargo, where employees opened 3.5 million deposit and credit card accounts without customers' consent in an effort to implement its now-infamous "cross-selling" strategy.[1]

The costs from that debacle were enormous, and the bank has yet to see the end of the financial carnage. In addition to paying millions in initial fines, reimbursing customers for fees, and eventually settling a class-action lawsuit to cover damages as far back as 2002, Wells Fargo has faced strong headwinds in attracting new retail customers. In recent years, more revelations about unauthorized mortgage modifications and fees, improper auto loan practices, and other missteps have surfaced. In February 2018 the Federal Reserve prohibited Wells Fargo from growing its assets any further until it strengthened its governance and risk management, and additional fines were levied by the Consumer Financial Protection Bureau and the Office of the Comptroller of the Currency a few months later. In the face of the bank's prolonged difficulties, the CEO who'd taken the helm after the scandal, Timothy Sloan, resigned in March 2019.

Were these devastating outcomes simply the natural consequences of having a bad strategy? Closer examination suggests that Wells Fargo never actually had a cross-selling *strategy*. It had a cross-selling *metric*. In its third quarter 2016 earnings report, the bank mentions an effort to "best align our cross-sell *metric* with our *strategic focus* of long-term retail banking relationships" [emphasis added].[2] In other words, Wells Fargo had—and still has—a strategy of building long-term customer relationships, and management intended to track the degree to which it was accomplishing that goal by measuring cross-selling. With brutal irony, a focus on the metric unraveled many of the bank's valuable long-term relationships.

Every day, across almost every organization, strategy is being hijacked by numbers, just as it was at Wells Fargo. It turns out that the tendency to mentally replace strategy with metrics—called *surrogation*—is quite pervasive. And it can destroy company value.

The Surrogation Snare

We all know that metrics are inherently imperfect at some level. In business the intent behind metrics is usually to capture some underlying intangible goal—and they almost always fail to do this as well as we would like. Your performance management system is full of metrics that are flawed proxies for what you care about.

Here's a common scenario: A company selects "delighting the customer" as a strategic objective and decides to track progress on it using customer survey scores. The surveys do tell managers something about how well the firm is pleasing customers, but somehow employees start thinking the strategy is to maximize survey scores, rather than to deliver a great customer experience.

It's easy to see how this could quickly become a problem, because there are plenty of ways to boost scores while actually displeasing customers. For example, what happened the last time you were urged to rate your experience a 10 on a satisfaction survey "because anything but a 10 is considered a failure"? That request may have turned negative feedback into a nonresponse or an artificially high score, and the pressure was probably off-putting. And think about all the pop-up windows, follow-up emails, and robocalls that pester you with surveys you would rather ignore. Such tactics tend to lower a customer's satisfaction with a company, but surrogation can lead those charged with delighting the customer to use them *despite* the strategy.

Surrogation is especially harmful when the metric and the strategy are poorly aligned. The greater the mismatch, the larger the potential damage. When a production manager's success at achieving the strategic objective to "make high-quality products" is measured by using very precise quality standards (such as "ball bearings must be 10 millimeters in diameter, plus or minus 0.0001 millimeters"), surrogation might not be a problem. However, if success at the objective is measured by the number of customer returns, the production manager might find creative ways to avoid returns. For example, they might connect directly with the purchasing departments of clientele, offering to personally handle any product concerns so that returns are registered as rework rather than returns. Or the manager might be willing to gamble a bit, pushing beyond acceptable (or even safe) quality standards, knowing that while the lower quality will increase the likelihood of a return, it may not actually trigger one. Furthermore, when a single metric is used more widely—for example, to gauge the performance of multiple managers overseeing various components of a complex product—surrogation can have a far bigger impact and do much greater harm.

Guarding Against Surrogation

To prevent surrogation, we must first understand how it happens. Two recent studies on surrogation—one using fMRI machines to measure blood flow in the brain to better understand how people make decisions, and the other using video games to examine surrogation in a nonbusiness setting—suggest that surrogation is a common subconscious bias: Whenever metrics are present, people tend to surrogate.[3] Nobel Prize–winner Daniel Kahneman and Yale professor Shane Frederick postulate that three conditions are necessary to produce the type of substitution we see with surrogation:

1. The objective or strategy is fairly abstract.

2. The metric of the strategy is concrete and conspicuous.

3. The employee accepts, at least subconsciously, the substitution of the metric for the strategy.

Multiple research studies have helped demonstrate how these conditions combine to produce surrogation. Knowledge of them supplies us with the means to combat the problem. Just as fire is stifled when the heat, fuel, or oxygen necessary for combustion is removed, surrogation can be suppressed by cutting off one or more of its key ingredients. Here's how to do that:

Get the people responsible for implementing strategy to help formulate it

This helps reduce surrogation because those involved in executing the strategy will then be better able to grasp it, despite its abstract nature—and to avoid replacing it with metrics. It's particularly crucial to bring the executives and senior managers who are charged with communicating strategy into this process. Research that one of us, Bill, did with Willie Choi of the University of Wisconsin and Gary Hecht of the University of Illinois, Urbana-Champaign, suggests that simply *talking* about strategy with people is not sufficient. In other words you can't just invite them to boardroom briefings and hang signs around the building promoting the strategy—you need to involve people in its development.

Consider the experiences of one organization Bill advised, Intermountain Healthcare. Its goal is to provide high-quality, low-cost care. One of the battlegrounds for this type of "value-based care" is the treatment of lower back pain. It turns out that most lower back pain goes away on its own in a few weeks. Medication and surgery can help, but they can also hurt—and they can be very costly. The data suggests that once a patient presents with lower back pain, the ideal response is to wait. So, with the involvement and advice of practicing physicians, Intermountain recently formulated a strategy aimed at reducing unnecessary interventions. To measure performance on the strategy, Intermountain began tracking whether doctors waited at least four weeks after meeting with a patient with lower back pain to recommend an X-ray, MRI, or another, more invasive diagnosis or treatment method.

The danger with this metric, of course, is that doctors could begin to see "make patients wait" as the objective rather than providing high-quality care at low cost. But because Intermountain doctors helped develop the strategy, this type of surrogation was far less likely to happen. And because the physicians were also heavily involved in the rollout and training for the strategy and its metrics, they could help others avoid surrogation as well. Indeed, Nick Bassett, executive director of population health at Intermountain, says that "without question, when physicians are involved in designing objectives, they better understand those objectives, and when they understand the objectives, they have proven time and time again their ability to determine the right course of action, often in spite of a particular metric."

Brett Muse, a doctor at Intermountain who played a large part in the strategy's development and rollout, agrees. "When I get in front of physicians and throw data at them, they get glassy-eyed," he says. Instead, he gets in front of the group and says, "Here's a problem involving quality of care. Let's try to solve this problem—and by the way, here's some data we can look at to see how we're doing."

Loosen the link between metrics and incentives

Tying compensation to a metric-based target tends to increase surrogation—an unfortunate side effect of pay for performance. Besides tapping into any monetary motivations people might have, this approach makes the metric much more visible, which means employees are more likely to focus on it at the expense of the strategy.

To think about how to get around this problem, let's look again at Intermountain's lower-back-pain metric. If management had done the obvious and just informed physicians that they would be paid a small bonus each time they required a patient to wait four weeks before receiving any costly tests or treatments, it probably would have driven even the most well-meaning doctors away from the true strategy of reducing unnecessary interventions and toward maximization of the metric. But the people overseeing the program didn't tie compensation to the metric, because they recognized that most doctors are already intrinsically motivated to provide high-value care. In addition, they set the target for the percentage of patients who waited four weeks before medical intervention at 80%. This served as a reminder to doctors that high-quality, low-cost care for *most* patients meant waiting for lower back pain to resolve itself, but for some patients—for example, those who waited a month before seeing the doctor in the first place—immediate treatment was warranted. The target reflected the imperfect nature of the metric and drew physicians' attention back to the underlying strategy.

Use multiple metrics

Another study Bill did with Choi and Hecht shows that people surrogate less when they're compensated for meeting targets on multiple metrics of a strategy rather than just one. This approach highlights the fact that no single metric completely captures the strategy, which makes people more likely to consciously reject substituting it for the strategy. At Intermountain overall physician performance is assessed with a myriad of metrics, including patient satisfaction, condition-specific quality metrics (such as average A1c levels of diabetes patients), health outcomes (such as hospital readmittance), preventive efforts (such as appropriately timed mammograms), and total cost of care. No lone metric is used to quantify the competence or contribution of the medical staff. Multiple yardsticks do add complexity to the task of performance evaluation, but they're essential to keeping people focused on the true strategy and avoiding surrogation.

Many managers learn the hard way that surrogation can spoil strategy, and if you don't take action to protect against it, it's very likely that sooner or later personal experience will lead you to the same realization. If you're using performance metrics, surrogation is probably already happening—the mere presence of a metric, even absent any compensation, is enough to induce some level of the behavior. So it's time to take a hard look internally to see which metrics might be most prone to surrogation and consider where it might cause the most damage.

———————

Michael Harris is a doctoral student at Duke University's Fuqua School of Business. **Bill Tayler** is the Robert J. Smith Professor at Brigham Young University's Marriott School of Business.

NOTES

1. Matt Egan, "Wells Fargo Uncovers up to 1.4 Million More Fake Accounts," CNN Business, August 31, 2017, https://money.cnn .com/2017/08/31/investing/wells-fargo-fake-accounts/index.html; Aaron Back, "Wells Fargo's Questionable Cross-Selling Strategy," *Wall Street Journal*, September 9, 2016, https://www.wsj.com/articles/ wells-fargos-questionable-cross-selling-strategy-1473444334.

2. Wells Fargo, "Wells Fargo Reports $5.6 Billion in Quarterly Net Income," press release, October 14, 2016, https://newsroom.wf.com/ press-release/corporate-and-financial/wells-fargo-reports-56-billion -quarterly-net-income.

3. Paul Black et al., "Surrogation Fundamentals: Measurement and Cognition," SSRN, July 12, 2018, https://papers.ssrn.com/sol3/ papers.cfm?abstract_id=3200074.

CHAPTER 19

The Two Types of Performance You Should Be Tracking

by Lindsay McGregor and Neel Doshi

Years ago Harvard Business School professor Ethan S. Bernstein studied assembly-line performance at a company he called "Precision."

Based in Southern China, Precision was the second-largest manufacturer of cell phones in the world at the time. Precision made it easy for managers to oversee

---

Adapted from "There Are Two Types of Performance—but Most Organizations Only Focus on One," on hbr.org, October 10, 2017 (product #H03Y0Z).

their employees. Every spot on every line was visible to managers. Every step of the process was measured, and real-time metrics were easily accessible. Workers were carefully trained to follow processes exactly as they were laid out.

But Bernstein and his team observed that when managers were not watching, employees secretly developed and shared better ways of doing the work. When Bernstein hid a set of production lines from managers' view, the performance of employees on those lines increased by 10% to 15%. It turns out that when employees felt that they were being monitored, they felt pressured to stick to "proven" methods. They couldn't adapt to improve their work.

Our research into over 20,000 workers of all skill levels across U.S. industries, and a review of hundreds of academic studies on the psychology of human performance, shows that most leaders and organizations tend to focus on just one type of performance. But there are two types that are important for success.

The first type is known as *tactical performance*. Tactical performance is how effectively your organization *sticks to* its strategy. It is the driver of focus and consistency. It allows organizations to increase strength by directing limited resources to the fewest targets. In Precision's case, good tactical performance required developing rules, checklists, and standard operating procedures and then following them closely. Similarly, when Starbucks baristas make your latte the same way across cafés, or when a software engineer delivers the expected features each sprint, you are witnessing tactical performance.

The second type, known as *adaptive performance*, is how effectively your organization *diverges* from its strategy. Adaptive performance manifests as creativity, problem-solving, grit, innovation, and citizenship. It allows organizations to create value in a world filled with, as the U.S. military says, volatility, uncertainty, complexity, and ambiguity, where technology and strategy changes rapidly. At Precision, good adaptive performance would have included every line worker coming up with new ideas and then teaching them to their colleagues. If you've ever seen a Starbucks barista adapt their greeting to make you feel personally welcome, or an engineer lean over to help a colleague solve an unexpected problem, you're witnessing adaptive performance.

Essentially, tactical performance is how well you stick to your plan, and adaptive performance is how well you diverge from it. Every high performer needs both. A great salesperson will operate much more efficiently with a defined process for reaching out to prospects. They will represent the products more consistently. But they must also adapt the standard approach based on each customer's unique needs. The same is true for any team or organization.

Overdoing Tactical Performance

If you've ever interacted with a customer representative who is clearly reading a script back to you, you're witnessing tactical performance destroying adaptive performance. The same happens when an engineer is tightly managed on their code velocity—in making sure to reach their goal, the engineer becomes far less likely to be creative or raise problems.

This is also true of executives. If you require them to post predictable earnings each quarter, they will reduce their investment in their companies' adaptive performance. Three finance professors once asked more than 400 executives what they would do if their quarterly earnings targets were at risk. Roughly 80% said they would cut back on spending in areas such as R&D; 55% said they would delay starting a new project, "even if this entails a small sacrifice in value."[1]

Of course, being too adaptive can also hurt tactical performance. For example, there are organizations that provide so much autonomy and freedom in how a process is executed that customers don't receive consistent experiences.

However, most companies measure only tactical performance. When we asked 2,823 American workers whether they have the ability to find new ways of working, only 27% agreed.

Building Balanced Cultures

In an experiment, we approached the call center of a bank's consumer loans business. (We've disguised some details of this story to protect confidential information.) This call center employed all the best practices of the day: A psychologist created scripts of talking points. Agents worked off an automatic phone-dialing computer ("the dialer") to ensure they had a customer to talk to every minute. Metrics emphasized speed. A stuffed monkey was placed on top of the cube of the worker who had collected the most revenue, to keep morale high. Weekly bonuses were given to employees who met a number of performance targets, including revenue earned, shorter duration of phone calls, and attaining the customer's email address. These stats were reviewed by managers every week.

Despite all of these systems encouraging tactical performance, productivity was trending downward and customer satisfaction had dropped off. Because the representatives feared losing their bonus if they did not follow standard scripts and operating procedures, they couldn't resolve customer problems that weren't in the script, and customers felt that they were talking to robots rather than human beings.

We asked the management team if we could eliminate the narrow metrics and bonuses, which rewarded only tactical performance, and focus more on the adaptive. The leadership team was skeptical that their teams would work without sticks or carrots, so they had us work with the lowest-performing employees in the building.

Our prior research had found that increasing employees' sense of play, purpose, and work potential can increase their adaptive performance, improving sales, customer experience, creativity, ethical behavior, and grit.[2] We made a number of operational changes to the call center.

First, we reduced tactical performance pressure. We ended the practice of agents taking the next phone call in line and instead gave them ownership over a set of customers. This increased their sense of purpose and meant they'd be able to go above and beyond for "their" people. We demoted calling scripts from "mandatory manuals" to "useful guides," reducing pressure to follow them. We rebuilt performance metrics to track impact, not to apply pressure. We eliminated pay-for-performance and gave each person a fair base salary equal to their average total earnings over the prior three months.

Next, we focused on increasing adaptive performance. We implemented weekly problem-solving meetings. Previously, working in the call center was a solo sport. Now, the team would get together weekly to raise tricky customer situations and come up with ideas for how to adapt. Guest experts from other parts of the business, from legal to marketing, were invited to visit when needed. The focus was on learning and adaptation—not on hitting performance goals.

We gave each team a quicker path to resolve unexpected problems while the customer was on the phone. Before, tricky problems would be redirected to a risk manager. It could take weeks for the risk manager to review the case. Now, a risk manager physically sat in between four teams. The customer service representatives could turn around and immediately work with the risk manager to solve a customer problem.

We also taught team leaders to focus on developing specific skills in agents, instead of just pointing out their deficiencies and bad behaviors. And we taught agents to invite others to join their phone calls when they thought a colleague's knowledge or service style would be a better fit for a particular customer. Finally, we taught the team to reflect on their performance routines on a regular basis so that they were constantly improving.

The change in performance was noticeable. Within four months, our pilot teams had more than doubled the close rates of the other teams. The pilot team made more adjustments to their approach, and members shared what worked more proactively with colleagues.

Building Adaptive Performance

When you find yourself saying things like "I wish my people took more ownership," "I wish we operated more like a startup," or "I wish we were more nimble," remember that most organizations have created so much emphasis on tactical performance that their people cannot adapt. Maintaining great performance over the long term will require organizations to also emphasize adaptive performance. These three steps can help:

Identify where you need tactical and adaptive performance

Hold a conversation with your team to understand where you need tactical performance and where you need adaptive. Tactical performance is required when you need consistency or scale—for example, every barista should follow the same recipe for a caramel macchiato, and every engineer should follow the same process for checking in code. Where you need tactical, ask if you've created the tools, checklists, and process flows that help you operate as efficiently as possible, freeing up some of your people's time to focus on being adaptive and improving their work.

Where you need adaptive performance, consider whether you've helped your people understand that it's OK to experiment. For example, do your people know that they can experiment with new ways of describing the latest coffee drink, or that it's OK to challenge the product design if an engineer has a better idea? Can you create routines, like the call center's problem-solving session, that teach your people how to experiment and adapt?

Implement metrics without myopia

A question we're frequently asked is "Does your research suggest we shouldn't give our people performance metrics?" Quite the contrary. People need to see information on their performance to self-correct. However, when you "weaponize" the data—linking it to high-stakes bonuses, promotions, and firing decisions—your people's adaptive performance will crumble. Instead, use the data to set learning goals. Start to measure the effectiveness of the conditions that affect adaptive performance, from how you motivate people to how you build your organization's structures, performance review systems, and planning processes.

Set learning goals

Imagine you're leading a sales team. You're working with one of your salespeople, and you noticed that they are selling five widgets per day, when the average for the rest of the team is eight widgets per day. It is very tempting as a manager to give that person a sales goal: "Your new goal is to sell eight widgets per day." From the perspective of the salesperson, they could work harder, take shortcuts or cheat, or take the time to learn how to perform better.

The learning route will lead to the ideal outcome. You could, for example, ask your salesperson to find five new ways of introducing the product to a prospective customer and note that you're not looking for five successful ways, just five new ways—and that it's OK to take some risks. Experiments have shown that setting learning goals produces results faster and more sustainably than only setting production goals.[3]

In sum, it's tempting to focus only on the tactical, to believe that to ensure success, all we need to do is track whether people follow the process. But high-performing organizations realize the world is full of volatility—and they need to prepare their people to adapt.

Lindsay McGregor and **Neel Doshi** are the coauthors of the *New York Times* bestseller *Primed to Perform,* and the cofounders and leaders of Vega and Factor, consulting and technology firms that help companies drive bottom-line performance and motivation.

NOTES

1. John Graham, Campbell Harvey, and Shiva Rajgopal, "The Economic Implications of Corporate Financial Reporting," *SSRN Electronic Journal* 40, no. 1–3 (2004): 3–73.

2. Lindsay McGregor and Neel Doshi, "How Company Culture Shapes Employee Motivation," hbr.org, November 25, 2015, "Introduction to Total Motivation," Vega Factor, video, n.d., https://www.vegafactor.com/introvideo/.

3. Dawn Winters and Gary P. Latham, "The Effect of Learning Versus Outcome Goals on a Simple Versus a Complex Task," *Group and Organization Management* 21, no. 2 (1996): 236–250.

CHAPTER 20

Making Silos Work for Your Organization

by Herman Vantrappen and Frederic Wirtz

Silos are a defining characteristic of organizations of all sizes, even in businesses that naturally operate as fluid networks. For example, management consulting firms are known for organizing around temporary project teams, but they also have formal expertise silos (often called practices) and fixed regional structures.

We often hear about the negative side effects of silos: Boundaries may lead to insular mindsets that inhibit sharing or collaboration between verticals, or worse,

---

Adapted from content posted on hbr.org, November 1, 2021 (product #H06OBF).

they could lead to finger-pointing and turf wars. The incitement to "bust" or "break down" silos appears frequently in both practitioner and scholarly journals.

But if silos are really such a bad thing, why then do they persist? Silos, or verticals, exist for three good reasons:

- **To aggregate expertise.** They provide the focus and critical mass required to develop expertise on an ongoing basis.

- **To assign accountability.** They provide boundaries and hierarchy that make it possible to assign accountability. Responsibilities are clearly delineated, objectives are well defined, resources are allocated firmly, and decisions are made and communicated quickly.

- **To provide a sense of identity.** They create stability and allow for the development of collective behavioral norms and ways of working. These, in turn, provide a sense of identity, security, psychological safety, and predictability for the people who belong to the silo.

As verticals serve a clear purpose, we would like to mount a defense. Yes, verticals have undesirable side effects, but the solution is not to dismantle them. To preserve the strengths of the inescapable verticals while minimizing their side effects, organizations should do two things: build bridges between verticals, and institute checks and balances.

Building Bridges

The topic of building bridges between verticals has already been well covered elsewhere.[1] Researchers André de Waal, Michael Weaver, Tammy Day, and Beatrice van der Heijden have identified four examples of how companies build bridges:[2]

- **Values.** A company's corporate values statement codifies the behavior that is expected from employees and can serve as an effective compass for all. By including "one company" behavior in its corporate values, a company signals that people should think and act beyond the boundaries of their verticals. It is no surprise that "collaboration" figures eminently in studies about frequently cited corporate values.[3]

- **Operating model.** People within a vertical know by routine how they should go about their daily work. But they may feel less secure and be reluctant to collaborate with people in other verticals. Such collaboration can be facilitated by hardwiring the interfaces between the verticals: defining clear procedures (for example, for approvals, consultation, and communication across boundaries) and providing an enabling infrastructure (for example, a common IT platform). Responsibility models, such as RACI, PACSI, and others, can help.

- **Community and people.** When building bridges, "softwiring" is as important as hardwiring.

Companies must create opportunities for people from different verticals to get to know one another's capabilities and interests, such as through joint training programs, cross-functional innovation initiatives, and companywide expert networks. Once familiarity is established, people will connect more easily whenever a concrete need for collaboration arises. Likewise, companies must pay attention to networking skills when recruiting people, designing training programs, considering sideways career moves, and measuring and rewarding performance.

- **Leadership.** The effectiveness of both hardwiring and softwiring depends on the company's leaders. They should have the skills and incentives to collaborate, for instance, by having performance indicators that measure the desired behaviors. They should demonstrate collaborative behavior themselves, for example, by showing loyalty to the joint decisions made in the management team.

As the list shows, bridges by and large call on the enlightened benevolence of people in different verticals. That may or may not work: While managers may genuinely acknowledge the benefits of collaboration, they still compete with one another for resources, senior management attention, and power.

This is where checks and balances enter the picture: They enable companies to minimize the side effects of verticals more forcefully than bridges do.

Checks and Balances

Let's first explain what we mean by checks and balances. A company's corporate objectives and key performance indicators (KPIs) reflect upper management and stakeholder expectations for revenues, profits, cash generation, ESG goals, and so on. These are then translated into vertical-specific objectives and KPIs that should be clear, motivational, and actionable. That exercise, however, is complicated by two phenomena:

- **Imperfect knowledge.** Managers of vertical A often must make decisions on the basis of knowledge that relates to matters in vertical B. But since their knowledge of vertical B is imperfect, they are bound to omit things and make mistakes. For instance, at one power company we worked with, the business development team had to make assumptions about the evolution of maintenance costs over the life cycle of the plant. While the best knowledge of those costs surely was within the maintenance department, we found that business development—out of ignorance, lack of time, or for other reasons—didn't inquire systematically with maintenance.

- **Partial optimization.** Managers of vertical A make choices to optimize their vertical's performance. Unfortunately, it may be the case that their choices are detrimental to the company's overall performance, either directly (because the corporate KPIs and the vertical's KPIs don't perfectly align) or indirectly (by affecting vertical B's performance negatively). For example, at the power company, the business development team decided to hire technical staff within its own vertical, as opposed to working with the corporate engineering team, thus reducing the latter's scale and overall performance. Or business development occasionally used less-experienced contractors, which led to hidden supervision costs down the road.

Checks and balances can mitigate these effects. Checks identify critical omissions, mistakes, and other lapses that a vertical may have made as a result of its imperfect knowledge of the subject matter. Balances act as circuit breakers when partial optimization threatens to damage the system in its entirety. Here are some examples of practical ways of instituting checks and balances:

- **Separate functions.** Transferring a function from one vertical to another changes its hierarchical reporting line and KPIs so that it is less constrained to do a fully objective job. For example, the power company's commercial-legal function was carved out from business development and attached to corporate legal to ensure that all legal aspects of a bid were duly considered.

- **Matrixed positions.** A wisely deployed matrix helps establish balance so that companies can change the reporting structures of certain roles.

For example, you could turn the role of the manager in charge of a function within vertical A into a matrix position—that is, make the manager also report to a supervisor within vertical B. Traditional corporate support functions (such as HR, finance, and legal) can play an important role in defining, rolling out, and supporting compliance of cross-vertical standards, policies, and methods—in particular, when the managers in charge of those functions are matrixed to the verticals *and* their corporate function. The power company we worked with assigned its commercial-technical manager to both business development *and* corporate engineering.

- **Governance.** Assign critical decisions requiring a cross-vertical purview to an existing or new cross-verticals body. For example, the power company instituted a new investment committee to review commercial tenders. Introduce thresholds to escalate approvals for decisions to an existing higher-level body as a function of their business impact and risks. If needed, make additional provisions such as veto rights or golden vote procedures.

- **Three-lines model.** From a control perspective, vertical managers are the so-called first line: They have the primary responsibility to achieve the objectives assigned to their vertical and manage the concomitant risks. But specific second-line functions (such as internal control, compliance, cybersecurity, sustainability, and risk) can provide assistance with managing risks, including the risk of having an insufficiently enterprise-wide perspective. Third-line functions (internal audit) provide additional checks and balances across verticals.

- **Intervention tools.** Institute ad hoc interventions using specific tools. The capital projects industry, for instance, uses a so-called assumptions book to ensure anticipation, explicitness, and transparency across verticals. Peer reviews by people from other verticals, shared "lessons learned" sessions, or third-party audits are other examples.

The boundaryless organization is a chimera. Verticals exist for good reasons: to aggregate expertise, assign accountability, and provide a sense of identity. To temper the attendant insular mindsets and behaviors, companies should build bridges between verticals and institute checks and balances carefully.

––––––––––

Herman Vantrappen is the managing director of Akordeon, a strategic advisory firm based in Brussels. He is the coauthor (with D. Deneffe) of the book *Fad-Free Strategy*. **Frederic Wirtz** heads The Little Group, advising companies on organization design issues worldwide.

NOTES

1. Xueming Luo, Rebecca J. Slotegraaf, and Xing Pan, "Cross-Functional 'Coopetition': The Simultaneous Role of Cooperation and

Competition Within Firms," *Journal of Marketing* 70, no. 2 (2018): 67–80.

2. André de Waal et al., "Silo-Busting: Overcoming the Greatest Threat to Organizational Performance," *Sustainability* 11, no. 23 (2019): 6860.

3. Donald Sull, Charles Sull, and Andrew Chamberlain, "Measuring Culture in Leading Companies," *MIT Sloan Management Review*, June 24, 2019, https://sloanreview.mit.edu/projects/measuring-culture-in-leading-companies/.

CHAPTER 21

How to Permanently Resolve Cross-Departmental Rivalries

by Ron Carucci

It can be challenging to synchronize complex tasks across multiple functions. Rather than cooperating, too many functions end up competing for power, influence, and limited resources. Such rivalry is more than a nuisance: It's costly.

Adapted from content posted on hbr.org, September 25, 2018 (product #H04JWE).

One study reports that 85% of workers experience some regular form of conflict, with U.S. workers averaging 2.8 hours per week.[1] That equates to $359 billion paid hours mired in conflict. It's easy to blame these conflicts on personalities (think toxic bosses or big egos), but in my experience as an organizational consultant, the root cause is more often systemic. For example, a study examining the rivalry between sales and marketing showed that conflicts between managers from these historically warring functions were not driven by interpersonal issues.[2] They were tied to the frequency of how they exchanged information, and the degree to which there were effective processes connecting their work.

When cross-departmental rivalries get heated and conflicts arise, I've frequently seen companies turn to team-building events or motivational speakers who talk about trust. But often these solutions aren't able to address the challenges these groups face because the organizational structure is *encouraging* these departments to dislike and distrust one another. For instance, I worked with a global consumer products company in which the commercial organization—the set of departments responsible for developing new products and bringing them to market—was deeply fragmented. There were misunderstandings across the group about what others did and sharp differences in how each subgroup defined a successfully commercialized product. R&D viewed operations as "the people who only know how to say no to opportunities," while operations viewed R&D as "the time- and money-wasters."

To better integrate and align rivaling functions, and therefore reduce friction and strengthen collaboration, leaders can address four critical questions that enable cross-functional teams to work together more coherently. These can happen over an extended working session or a series of conversations. (For more on leading discussions between rivaling teams, see the sidebar "Being a Collaborative Leader.")

What value do we create together?

The seams that connect major functions are where a company's greatest competitive distinctions lie. Discrete technical capabilities reside within functions, but when blended with the capabilities of adjacent functions, they combine into capabilities that drive performance. But that value is only realized when those functions understand their shared contributions for creating it. In my client example, the people in R&D and operations came to see one another differently, and work more collaboratively, because they realized that their combined expertise was necessary to get products to market faster. Neither alone controlled speed to market, but together they could significantly influence it. R&D needed to be disciplined in how they provided product specifications to manufacturing, and operations needed to be adaptable in order to accommodate new products they'd never had to make before. Marketing and R&D's combined value could be creating innovations that prioritize the customer. By identifying which objectives in the organization's strategy the functions mutually contribute to, they

BEING A COLLABORATIVE LEADER

by Rebecca Newton

Collaborative leadership has been identified as a fundamental differentiator in achieving strategic objectives. To make a difference though, it has to go beyond the polite, thoughtful behaviors of involving others, sharing information, and lending strength when it's needed. Real collaborative leadership is facilitating constructive interpersonal connections and activities between heterogenous groups to achieve shared goals. It is proactive and purpose-driven.

When it comes to being a collaborative leader, these tips can help drive success:

- *Focus on interests rather than positions.* As with negotiations and conflict resolution, one of the most important keys to successful collaborative leadership is focusing on interests rather than positions. Participants may have different positions, yet common ground can almost always be found at the level of interests. In collaborating with others, ask, "What's most important to you here? What really matters?" Encourage their openness and foster trust by sharing personally what your main drivers are.

- *Be an agent and a target of influence.* We spend a lot of time in leadership development helping professionals to have greater influence.

Of equal importance is being prepared to be a *target* of others' influence. This requires *openness* to alternative ideas; *inquisitiveness* to understand the foundation of others' arguments; and *recognition* of the value the other party has and therefore can add to the collaborative venture.

- *Define clear roles and responsibilities.* Research has shown that where leaders are successfully leading together, they have a clear sense of who is responsible for what. Mapping out these roles and responsibilities early, and refining them along the collaborative journey, ensures a smoother road.

- *Share and acknowledge credit.* We know that acknowledging our own part in a problem, even if it's taking only 5% of the blame, alleviates tension during conflict and leads to faster reconciliation. The reverse is true of facilitating collaborative success. Acknowledging others' contributions—whether they are big or small—in the success of our ventures energizes them in our collaborative efforts.

- *Have a mission worthy of collaboration.* For collaborative leadership to be purposeful and

(*continued*)

BEING A COLLABORATIVE LEADER

sustainable, it needs to meet all parties' true interests, warrant their time, and help them achieve their core objectives. Leaders need to highlight why this particular collaboration matters, what difference it will make, and encourage the project's participants to create the time and space in their schedules that it deserves.

Rebecca Newton is an organizational and psychologist and senior visiting fellow at the London School of Economics and Political Science and a faculty member on executive education programs at Harvard Law School. Rebecca is the CEO of leadership consulting firm CoachAdviser and author of *Authentic Gravitas: Who Stands Out and Why*.

Adapted from "Collaborate Across Teams, Silos, and Even Companies," on hbr.org, July 25, 2014 (product #H00X5L).

---

reduce the perception of conflicting goals. They also better manage the healthy, natural tensions between objectives like containing cost and investing in opportunities that may not materialize.

What capabilities do we need to deliver the value?

Having anchored their relationship in creating value for the company together, groups can now focus on how best to achieve it. Functions should identify the four to five critical shared capabilities they must have. These may include the translation of market analytics into product opportunities, technical problem-solving, or the fast and accurate exchange of information and learning as projects move through the development process. Identifying these requires an honest assessment of the organization to uncover any lagging or missing capabilities or processes that best integrate each function's efforts. In the case of my client, we discovered there was no forum to bring together all of the commercial functions—regulatory, packaging, manufacturing, and marketing—to discuss potential problems with ongoing projects. As a result, information was slow to get to decision makers and was often distorted by the time it did. The organization created a monthly meeting for these groups to come together to discuss challenges and solve problems with greater candor.

How will we resolve conflicts and make decisions while maintaining trust?

Conflicts will inevitably come up when trying to better coordinate efforts. Answering this question together presents an opportunity to "rehearse" those conflicts in advance. Functions should identify the critical decisions they'll need to make in pursuit of their cocreated value and determine who gets to make the final call on those decisions. This requires acknowledging any historical baggage or unresolved distrust between the functions. Only when those concerns are fully aired can any biases people have toward one another's department be removed. Empathy is key here, as is sharing information on what it's like to interact with one another. I've often heard people express during this part of the conversation sentiments like, "I had no idea you guys had to do that! No wonder our requests annoy you!" The goal is to increase the respect the departments have for one another and build greater commitment to collective success.

What do we need from each other to succeed?

This final question is about supporting one another's work going forward. Groups must create detailed service-level agreements to one another and negotiate things like time lines of information sharing, quality standards, how far in advance notification is needed for changes, and how day-to-day work will be coordinated. The departments may need to share access to particular technology platforms or include people from other groups in certain meetings so that they get the information they need and provide input at the right time. Once the group agrees on which commitments they need to make, they must stick to them.

Organizations naturally fragment as they grow, pulling people apart into silos and creating functional borders that can set rivalry in motion. If you see fraying cross-functional relationships, don't resort to superficial solutions like team building or conflict training. Dig deeper to understand what's really causing those fractions and take steps together to set up your functions for mutual success.

Ron Carucci is a cofounder and managing partner at Navalent, working with CEOs and executives pursuing transformational change. He is the bestselling author of eight books, including *To Be Honest* and *Rising to Power*. Download his free "How Honest is My Team?" assessment at www.tobehonest.net/assessment.

NOTES

1. CPP, "Workplace Conflict and How Businesses Can Harness It to Thrive," CPP Global Human Capital Report, July 2008, https://kilmanndiagnostics.com/wp-content/uploads/2018/04/CPP_Global_Human_Capital_Report_Workplace_Conflict.pdf.

2. Philip L. Dawes and Graham R. Massey, "Antecedents of Conflict in Marketing's Cross-Functional Relationship with Sales," *European Journal of Marketing*, November 2005.

When Your Strategy Needs to Change

CHAPTER 22

When Shifting Strategy, Don't Lose Sight of Your Long-Term Vision

by Ron Ashkenas

Given the time and effort it takes to develop and execute new strategies, it's best not to introduce them too often. But there are instances when short-term strategic shifts are unavoidable—especially in today's ever-changing business context. Take, for example, the need to respond to calls for social change or demands from investors to turn around poor financial results.

Adapted from content posted on hbr.org, June 2, 2022 (product #H0728N).

When responding to these kinds of pressures, executives must take care to align the strategic shifts they introduce with the larger picture of where their organization is heading and what it aspires to accomplish in the future—the company's "vision." After all, strategy—overarching decisions about priorities and resource allocations—should be all about translating that vision into action. When vision and strategy are at odds, employees, shareholders, and customers may lose confidence that management has a coherent and consistent plan for moving the company forward.

To achieve this alignment, executives need to evaluate whether proposed short-term strategic shifts are consistent with the longer-term vision and resist the pressure to take on those strategies that run counter to it. (To help you identify when your strategy might need to shift, see the sidebar "When Should You Switch Strategy?") This process itself can help leaders assess whether their vision is sufficiently clear and compelling or may need to be sharpened or revised.

Let's look at how this plays out in different contexts in practice.

Responding to Social Change

Connecting short-term strategic responses to a long-term vision is particularly important when companies are responding to social movements. These can put pressure on companies to act quickly and publicly. But when company leaders implement strategies that aren't tied to a larger vision, those strategies can wither on the vine.

For example, in the summer of 2020, after the murder of George Floyd, many firms raced to come up with

WHEN SHOULD YOU SWITCH STRATEGY?

by Mark Chussil

Don't assume you should change your competitive strategy only because something has changed and the knee-jerk, do-something alarm is roaring. Companies rightly seek agility and fear complacency. But consider the flip side: The more zealously you monitor the world, the more likely you will react to noise instead of signal. And this: The better your current strategy, the more likely a new strategy will be worse.

Here are other factors to consider:

- If you expect market conditions to be significantly different for a prolonged period, you should be more open to a new strategy than if you expect smaller, shorter effects. Be more open to switch, not precommitted to switch.

- If you suspect structural changes in your market, consider strategy changes. Estimate, calculate, or simulate whether you should risk a false-positive mistake (acting because you think something is real) or a false-negative mistake (not acting because you think something is ephemeral).

- If you feel the weight of the managerial imperative to do something, pause before you obey. For example, does the situation present opportunities better than slashing costs and prices? Should you assume the market will eventually

(continued)

WHEN SHOULD YOU SWITCH STRATEGY?

return to "normal"? Should you act to accelerate the shift to a new normal?

- If you're unhappy with your current strategy's performance or prospects, ask yourself why a potential new strategy would improve results. In my business war games I've seen companies discover that new, "obvious" strategies could lead to disaster.

- Remember that doing nothing is always an option. I'm not saying you *should* do nothing, but it's good analytic practice to consider the option.

Mark Chussil is the founder and CEO of Advanced Competitive Strategies. He has conducted business war games, taught strategic thinking, and written strategy simulators for *Fortune* 500 companies around the world.

Adapted from "When to Switch Strategy in a Crisis," on hbr.org, February 3, 2021 (product #H063JW).

strategies to convince their people and their customers that they stood firm against systemic racism. But the results of their efforts have been decidedly mixed. While some have pointed to the inefficacy of widely implemented anti-racism training as the culprit, I believe that these strategies fell short of their companies' rhetoric because they were not supported by a larger vision of how the companies themselves needed to change.

In contrast, for companies that already had a robust vision for building inclusion and diversity, their new strategies were supported by a preexisting framework and have proved more successful. At Johnson & Johnson, for example, by the summer of 2020, the pharmaceutical firm already had a detailed vision—"to maximize the global power of diversity and inclusion, to drive superior business results and sustainable competitive advantage"—and was actively engaged in initiatives that would move the company in this direction.[1] So in November 2020, when J&J responded to the increasing awareness of social injustice by pledging $100 million to address racism and health inequities, the strategy—which included support for mobile health clinics in communities of color, and a 50% increase in hiring people of color into leadership positions in J&J—was clearly part of an ongoing commitment and not a onetime, knee-jerk response to social pressure. This consistency is perhaps one reason that employees from often-marginalized categories feel highly positive about the company's culture and work environment, putting it in the top 10% of companies with over 10,000 employees on Comparably, a workplace rating site.[2]

Leaders whose companies feel compelled to take immediate strides in response to social action should consider whether they have this kind of longer-term vision in place as well. (See the sidebar "Check Your Vision.") If not, they should develop that vision in parallel with

CHECK YOUR VISION

Aligning your strategy with your long-term vision presupposes that you have one. But that's something you should test—especially when you are faced with the pressure to change your strategy.

A quick way to do this is to first ask yourself how, in the next three to five years, your company (or department or unit) will set itself apart from the competition, attract great talent, and be financially or operationally sustainable. Put this down on paper in no more than a few sentences. Then ask three of your direct reports and a few other stakeholders (like a board member, a key customer, or a partner) to answer the same question.

If you can't articulate the vision easily, or you don't get a reasonably consistent response from others, then either you don't have a clear and exciting vision or it hasn't been well communicated or understood.

If indeed your vision doesn't pass this test, then take some time (even if it's just a few days) to clarify the longer-term vision. Putting your long-term vision front and center is a critical first step for incorporating short-term strategic shifts into your plans.

their more immediate strategies. PepsiCo's response in the summer of 2020 was future- and big-picture focused in this way. The company vowed to add 100 nonwhite associates to its executive ranks within five years and, as of 2022, achieved at least a quarter of that goal. The company also said that it would double its spending with Black-owned suppliers in five years and has made tangible progress in that direction.

Responding to Business Pressure

Aligning short-term strategies with a longer-term vision also is critical in responding to financial pressures, as executives often feel like they have no choice about pursuing change when the numbers demand it.

A case in point is GE, which, starting in 2005, had a compelling, long-term vision for reducing environmental impact at a global scale called "ecoimagination." This vision drove GE toward investments in wind and water and initiatives to lower carbon emissions technologies for jet engines and other products. The vision was generally well received. But the pressure to maintain and grow revenues led GE to a strategy of selling the water business in 2017 and doubling down on acquisitions in the nonrenewable energy sector (see, for example, the $9.5 billion 2015 purchase of Alstom's power business, including the manufacture of coal-fueled turbines, and the 2016 merger with Baker Hughes, which provides services and equipment for oil drilling). These deals gave lie to GE's green image and mired the company with an unmanageable debt load—problems that could possibly have been avoided by staying true to ecoimagination.

In contrast, Merck CEO Ken Frazier kept his company's actions focused squarely on the company's ultimate vision despite immense pressure in the early 2010s from shareholders to cut back on research and development as a strategy for increasing profitability and share price. Frazier pushed back on that strategic shift and even budgeted *more* for R&D because he saw it as key to the company's long-term vision to "use the power of leading-edge science to save and improve lives around the world."[3] Despite taking short-term heat for his decision, Frazier kept the company focused on the vision—a strategy that led to the development and approval of a blockbuster immuno-oncology drug, a robust research pipeline, and by the time Frazier retired in 2021, a stock price that had more than doubled.

Use Change to Accelerate Your Vision

No matter where the pressure to change your strategy comes from, think not only about whether you can align the changes with long-term vision but also how you can do it in a way that *accelerates* your company's pursuit of that vision.

For example, a large technology firm that had a long-term goal of attracting more women to its high-tech jobs used the abrupt move to remote and hybrid work as a way of proactively speeding up its gender diversity vision. From previous studies and observations, executives at the company had realized that women, who still bore the brunt of childcare, often had a hard time breaking into the company's on-site tech teams where men stayed late or went out together after work; and that many women valued flexible work hours more than camaraderie. Driven by these insights, they intentionally leveraged the lessons from the remote and hybrid work arrangements necessitated by the Covid-19 pandemic to make the colocated office teams less essential; and they are empowering managers to continue creating flexible work arrangements for both new and current employees. Although it's too soon to know for sure, early indications across the industry are that this is making it easier to recruit and retain women.[4]

When considering a change in strategy, don't just look at the immediate situation. Think of the long term. Without a vision to guide you, responsive strategic shifts will get you somewhere, but not necessarily where you want to go.

Ron Ashkenas is a coauthor of the *Harvard Business Review Leader's Handbook* and a partner emeritus at Schaffer Consulting. His previous books include *The Boundaryless Organization, The GE Work-Out,* and *Simply Effective.*

NOTES

1. Kiely Kuligowski, "6 Examples of Diverse and Inclusive Companies," *Business News Daily*, January 23, 2023, https://www.businessnewsdaily.com/15970-diverse-inclusive-companies.html.

2. "Diversity at Johnson & Johnson," *Comparably*, n.d., https://www.comparably.com/companies/johnson-johnson/diversity.

3. Merck, "Merck's Q4 and Full-Year 2022 Earnings Report," https://www.merck.com/stories/mercks-q4-and-full-year-2022-earnings-report/.

4. Owen Hughes, "Tech Jobs Are Booming, and Hybrid Working Sees More Women Join the Industry," ZDNET, November 17, 2021, https://www.zdnet.com/article/tech-jobs-are-booming-and-hybrid-working-sees-more-women-join-the-industry/.

CHAPTER 23

How to Adapt Your Strategy When Crisis Hits

by Michael Wade, Amit Joshi, and Elizabeth A. Teracino

In early 2020, Airbnb was headed for a banner year—bookings were up, expansion plans were in place, and an IPO was set for the spring. Then Covid-19 hit, and more than $1 billion of bookings disappeared, expansion plans were postponed, and one-quarter of the workforce was cut. However, by the end of the year, revenues had recovered, and the company completed one of the most successful tech IPOs in history.[1]

Adapted from "6 Principles to Build Your Company's Strategic Agility," on hbr.org, September 2, 2021 (product #H06K1X).

Ultimately Airbnb and other companies that successfully navigated the crisis were able to deviate from their strategic plan and adapt to the changing environment. Our research identified three distinct ways they did this:

1. They were nimble enough to *avoid* the worst impacts.

2. They were robust enough to *absorb* a lot of the damage when they were hit.

3. They were resilient enough to *accelerate* forward faster and more effectively than their peers.

We refer to this combination of capabilities as the Triple A's of strategic agility.

As soon as it became clear that travel restrictions would be inevitable, Airbnb took steps to *avoid* impact to its business. It implemented strict disinfectant protocols for its properties and added a mandatory free night between stays to allow additional time for cleaning. It also relaxed guest cancellation policies and put measures in place to compensate hosts for lost revenue. Of course, the company couldn't entirely avoid the effects of the pandemic, so it raised capital to bolster its ability to *absorb* the impact of reduced bookings and cancellations. Even before the business was stabilized, the company began to *accelerate* into areas that were less affected, such as in-country travel and stays at rural locations. It also started to promote longer "quarantine" stays and added details such as internet speed to its listings.

The Six Principles Behind a Triple-A Rating

Strategic agility is the ability to improve performance—not just survive but thrive—amid disruption. Our multi-year research project, based on studying qualitative and quantitative data from hundreds of organizations, suggests that strategic agility can be further broken down into six principles. These principles are not definitions, rules, laws, tools, or frameworks, but guidelines to help organizations leverage disruption proactively to their advantage.

Avoiding shocks

Sidestepping shocks is linked to sensing risks in the environment, being able to position yourself to avoid dangers, and moving quickly to dodge impacts.

Principle 1: Prioritize speed over perfection

Opportunities come and go quickly during a crisis, so organizations need to be ready and willing to act quickly, even if they sacrifice quality and predictability in the process.

During the multiday celebration of Chinese New Year, movie theaters are typically full of families. However, in January 2020, due to the spread of Covid-19, most theaters were empty, and many had closed their doors. The Huanxi Media Group stood to lose millions on its New Year's–themed movie *Lost in Russia*.

While most of its peers decided to postpone their releases, Huanxi approached ByteDance, the Chinese company behind the blockbuster app TikTok. ByteDance was not an obvious distribution partner, as its properties stream mostly short-form, user-generated content. For instance, at the time, TikTok capped videos at 15 seconds—and *Lost in Russia* clocked in at over two hours.

In just two days, *Lost in Russia* racked up 600 million views on ByteDance platforms. Not only did the movie gain a huge following, but it also led to a flood of goodwill from Chinese citizens who were frustrated about not being able to leave their homes during the outbreak. By waiting, other studios missed out on a major opportunity to build market share and capitalize on a limited-term opportunity.

Principle 2: Prioritize flexibility over planning

Strategy is often taught in business schools as a cascade of choices around where to play and how to win. These choices are typically built into strategic plans that are devised and approved over a period of several months and then executed over three or five years, before the cycle repeats. However, in a crisis, a strategic plan can easily become an anchor that locks an organization onto a path that is no longer relevant.

Faced with a massive drop in revenue during the pandemic, Qantas abandoned its five-year strategic plan and dusted off an old idea from the 1980s to offer "flights to nowhere." These excursions included flybys of some of Australia's main tourist destinations, such as the Great Barrier Reef and Uluru. The entire stock of seats sold out in 10 minutes, making it the fastest-selling promotion in Qantas's history.

Qantas was not only quick off the mark but flexible in how it operated. The airline recognized the public's latent desire to travel, even if they couldn't leave the country, and it quickly adapted its services to meet this need. It then built on its initial success, next offering viewing flights to Antarctica.

Absorbing shocks

When it's impossible to avoid a shock, the next best thing is to minimize the damage. This step is often misunderstood by managers. Some of the hallmarks of strong shock absorption—scale, inefficiency, or centralization—are seen as impediments to effective competition in volatile environments. Yet, when set up in the right way, these elements can enhance the ability of organizations to withstand shocks without inhibiting performance.

Principle 3: Prioritize diversification and "efficient slack" over optimization

Many organizations struggled—and some failed—during the pandemic not because they weren't nimble or innovative, but because they were felled by a single devastating blow. The root of this problem, in many cases, was either a lack of diversification or an overemphasis on efficiency and optimization.

The principles of diversification and slack have fallen out of favor recently. The share price of diversified organizations is often hit with a "conglomerate discount," and markets and activist investors are quick to penalize any sign of slack. Yet, these are both powerful hedges against the impact of shocks. Pain in one area can be compensated by gain elsewhere. During the pandemic, when sales in P&G's personal care brands dropped, the company was able to make up the difference in increased revenue of its cleaning and disinfectant brands. By contrast, Gold's Gym, Avianca Airlines, and Brooks Brothers suffered from a lack of diversification and ultimately went bankrupt.

Swiggy, one of India's largest food-delivery startups, built a platform that included more than 160,000 restaurants in 500 cities. During the Covid-19 lockdown, restaurant activity, including deliveries, fell by more than 50%. Swiggy realized that its overdependence on fixed-location, traditional "sit down" restaurants as delivery partners was a severe vulnerability. In response, it started a program to add street food vendors to its platform, ultimately adding more than 36,000 of these vendors. While servicing the vendors was less profitable, they provided valuable slack during the crisis, while also delivering a societal benefit. As a consequence, the company rebounded to about 90% of its pre-Covid-19 food-delivery volumes.

Principle 4: Prioritize empowerment over hierarchy

Systems are most vulnerable at their weakest points. A hierarchy, for example, is most vulnerable at the top.

Empowered teams, by contrast, are inherently robust. Since they're decentralized, no single strike or crisis can take them all out. The key is to maintain open and regular information flows so that they are working from the same page.

Zoetis, a leading global health company for animals, adopted this approach during the pandemic, which arrived just as it was about to launch its largest ever new product, a medication for dogs. A number of challenges, including supply-chain disruptions, marketing delays, and reduced opening hours at testing centers and laboratories, threatened to scupper the launch. In response, Zoetis's CEO decided to allow local leaders across 45 global markets autonomy to conduct the launch in the most appropriate way. For example, social-distancing regulations varied massively by location, as did requirements to wear protective clothing. The empowerment extended to field-based employees, managers, and teams who were encouraged to "run it like you own it." To further enable these employees, a priority was placed on data-driven decision-making, and dashboards containing up-to-the-minute information on the pandemic were made available to everyone in the organization.

Accelerating away from shocks

Bouncing back from shocks is partially operational (being able to redeploy and reconfigure resources) and partially cultural (fostering a tolerance for failure and implementing an environment that encourages risk-taking and rewards learning). The application of the acceleration principles has a major impact on performance in highly uncertain environments.

Principle 5: Prioritize learning over blaming

It has been well established that organizational cultures that reward risk-taking and tolerate failure move more quickly that those that don't.[2] If people are criticized for failing, they are less likely to take risks; in a crisis, this can be fatal.

Evalueserve is a midsize global IT services firm with offices in India. When the country declared a strict lockdown with six hours' notice, it had no choice but to shift almost all of its 3,000 employees to work from home. This move created an increased risk to employee well-being and morale, as home environments were often stressful and not conducive for working. In response, the company instituted several changes to promote a "no blame" culture. It added mental health and well-being initiatives such as "no agenda check-in calls" to maintain motivation, as chair Timo Vättö and cofounder Marc Vollenweider explained to us in an interview. The company also adjusted its incentives to reward employees for learning and adaptability. As a result, Evalueserve faced negligible attrition of both employees and clients during the lockdown.

Principle 6: Prioritize resource modularity and mobility over resource lock-in

Since it is difficult to predict how the future will unfold in a crisis, it is hard to effectively plan the allocation of resources. Thus, it's important to build resources that are modular and/or mobile so that they can be reconfigured or moved as needed.

An example of resource modularity comes from the "Paranoid Fan" app, which allowed NFL fans to order food to be delivered to their seats in sports stadiums. But with live events curtailed by the pandemic, the app lost its users. Seeing long queues outside food banks in New York City, founder Agustin Gonzalez recognized an opportunity to reconfigure the app's mapping and delivery technology. The company launched a new app, named Nepjun, that allowed food banks to set menus and create delivery protocols, while also allowing users to find operational food banks in their neighborhood.

Putting Strategic Agility into Action

The year 2020 was an extremely disruptive one for the media and entertainment sector. Streaming companies like Netflix and Amazon Prime Video experienced strong growth, while organizations involved in live events and cinematic releases suffered massive drops in revenue. The Walt Disney Company was caught in the middle. In early 2020, media and broadcasting operations accounted for about a third of its revenue, 17% was earned from direct-to-consumer brands, and the remaining 50% came from movie studios, theme parks, and product sales.

Gains in broadcasting revenues failed to offset heavy losses from the closure of movie theaters, theme parks, and retail stores. Disney's share price began 2020 at $146, but by March 20 it had dropped to $86 a share as the global scale of the pandemic became apparent. The company managed to *avoid* the worst impacts of the pandemic for as long as it could by keeping its theme parks open in a limited capacity and adding strong safety protocols for all facilities, staff, and guests. It saved money by laying off employees across its portfolio of stores, parks, and cruise ships, and worked with local governments where possible to supplement its income. A strong balance sheet allowed it to *absorb* the drop in revenue.

Meanwhile, the company reallocated resources and people to its Disney+ streaming service that had been launched in November 2019. The company worked hard to *accelerate* enhancements to the offering, adding new content throughout the year. For example, the live-action cinematic release *Mulan* was offered through the service as a special paid feature. By the end of the year, the company had attracted more than 90 million paying subscribers to the Disney+ service, significantly outperforming competitors such as HBO Max and Peacock, and far exceeding a goal it had hoped to meet by 2024.[3]

When conditions improved, Disney was quick to take advantage. It reopened its theme parks in Shanghai in May and Tokyo in July. Most important, it continued to heavily invest in Disney+, building it into one of the world's largest video subscription services just a year after launch. It empowered local managers to make decisions as situations shifted across the world, and it moved people and resources around to focus on growing areas. Its story shows that even large companies that are in the firing line of shocks like Covid-19 can respond effectively as long as they leverage the Triple A's of strategic agility.

While the Covid-19 crisis was a unique event, there is no doubt that organizations will continue to face other challenging situations in the future. Under these circumstances, incorporating avoidance, absorption, and acceleration can be the difference between survival and collapse.

——————

Michael Wade is a professor of innovation and strategy at IMD and holds the Cisco Chair in Digital Business Transformation. He is a coauthor of *ALIEN Thinking: The Unconventional Path to Breakthrough Ideas*. **Amit Joshi** is a professor of AI, analytics, and marketing strategy and the director of the Digital Excellence Diploma at IMD. **Elizabeth A. Teracino** is a postdoctoral researcher and lecturer at the Faculty of Business and Economics at the University of Lausanne and a senior researcher in the Competence Center Corporate Data Quality.

NOTES

1. Bobby Allyn and Avie Schneider, "Airbnb Now a $100 Billion Company After Stock Market Debut Sees Stock Price Double," NPR, December 10, 2020, https://www.npr.org/2020/12/10/944931270/airbnb-defying-pandemic-fears-takes-its-company-public-in-ipo.

2. Amy C. Edmondson and Per Hugander, "4 Steps to Boost Psychological Safety at Your Workplace," hbr.org, June 22, 2021, https://hbr.org/2021/06/4-steps-to-boost-psychological-safety-at-your-workplace.

3. Sarah Whitten, "Disney+ Tops 100 Million Subscribers Just 16 Months After Launch," CNBC, March 9, 2021, https://www.cnbc.com/2021/03/09/disney-tops-100-million-subscribers-just-16-months-after-launch.html.

Index

Smart advice and inspiration from a source you trust.

If you enjoyed this book and want more comprehensive guidance on essential professional skills, turn to the HBR Guides Boxed Set. Packed with the practical advice you need to succeed, this seven-volume collection provides smart answers to your most pressing work challenges, from writing more effective emails and delivering persuasive presentations to setting priorities and managing up and across.

Harvard Business Review Guides

Available in paperback or ebook format. Plus, find downloadable tools and templates to help you get started.

- Better Business Writing
- Building Your Business Case
- Buying a Small Business
- Coaching Employees
- Delivering Effective Feedback
- Finance Basics for Managers
- Getting the Mentoring You Need
- Getting the Right Work Done

- Leading Teams
- Making Every Meeting Matter
- Managing Stress at Work
- Managing Up and Across
- Negotiating
- Office Politics
- Persuasive Presentations
- Project Management

HBR.ORG/GUIDES

Buy for your team, clients, or event.
Visit hbr.org/bulksales for quantity discount rates.

Notes

Notes

Notes

Notes

Notes

Notes

Notes